D1559663

# The History and Theology
## of
# SOKA
# GAKKAI

## A Japanese New Religion

## DANIEL METRAUX

Studies in Asian Thought and Religion
Volume 9

The Edwin Mellen Press
Lewiston/Queenston

**Library of Congress Cataloging-in-Publication Data**

Metraux, Daniel Alfred.
    The history and  theology of Soka Gakkai: a Japanese new religion/
Daniel A. Metraux.
        p. cm. -- (Studies in Asian thought and religion; v. 9)
    Bibliography: p.
    Includes index.
    ISBN 0-88946-055-8
    1. Soka Gakkai. I. Title. II. Series.
BQ8415.4.M48  1988                                              88-1613
294.3'928--dc19                                                 CIP

This is volume 9 in the continuing series
Studies in Asian Thought and Religion
Volume 9 ISBN 0-88946-055-8
SATR Series ISBN 0-88946-050-7

The Edwin Mellen Press                    The Edwin Mellen Press
Box 450                                              Box 67
Lewiston, New York                    Queenston, Ontario
USA 14092                                    L0S 1L0 CANADA

Printed in the United States of America

# The History and Theology
## of
# SOKA
# GAKKAI

## A Japanese New Religion

# TABLE OF CONTENTS

# PREFACE

The Soka Gakkai is a unique phenomenon in modern Japanese history. No other modern religious organization has succeeded in creating such a widespread social movement on the foundation of Buddhist ideals. In forty years the movement has spread throughout Japan and to nearly one hundred other countries, and it claims a following of about ten million. Critics of the Soka Gakkai doubt its permanence, but the Gakkai is far more than a temporary phenomenon.

The Soka Gakkai's goal is to reform society on the basis of its view of Buddhism. Gakkai leaders claim to have the one religious philosophy that can bring peace, harmony, and happiness to mankind, and they regard it as their supreme duty to propagate their version of the teachings of Nichiren throughout the world. They insist that sincere converts will experience an immediate reformation of character that will lead them to become generous, loving, and peaceful beings. Society itself will improve when many people become believers.

The purpose of this work is to present an eschatological profile of the Soka Gakkai. The Gakkai asserts that man today lives in a world replete with violence, misery, and apathy, but that a far happier and more peaceful world can be attained if man will put the Gakkai doctrines into practice. The world view of the Soka Gakkai is examined through an analysis of the following: its own historical development; its interpretation of the social views of its founder, Nichiren; the motivation for membership; its activities in Japan and abroad.

I wish to acknowledge the help and cooperation of Soka Gakkai Presidents Ikeda and Akiya, Vice Presidents Yamazaki and Kirimura, as well as Akiyama Tomiya,[1] Director of the Soka Gakkai's International Bureau and his entire staff including his deputy, Yamaguchi Hiromu. I wish to express my deep gratitude to the Ministry of Education of Japan for its generous support of the first phase of this research and to numerous other Japanese scholars whose help and guidance was invaluable. Finally, I wish to thank Mary Baldwin College for its support, Beverly Askegaard for her careful editing, and my wife and children who had to endure my many changes of mood and considerable loneliness as this work was in progress.

Daniel A. Metraux
Staunton, Virginia
Summer, 1987

---

1. All Japanese names are presented in the traditional Japanese order with last names first.

# CHAPTER 1

## ESCHATOLOGY IN JAPANESE BUDDHISM: THE WORLD VIEW OF NICHIREN AND THE SOKA GAKKAI

People watching the Japanese film <u>Ningen Kakumai</u> (The Human Revolution)[1] are treated to a series of spectacular scenes depicting death and destruction in thirteenth century Japan. At the start of the movie, there are fires and havoc everywhere: earthquakes send whole mountainsides down on helpless villages, and fierce soldiers cross the countryside fighting one another and killing innocent civilians. The viewer next sees pictures of Japan's devastation during World War II. Whole sections of Tokyo and other cities are destroyed leaving thousands of homeless, dazed people to wander around seeking food and shelter with little success. There is not a happy face to be seen anywhere.

A Soka Gakkai vice-president, Yamazaki Hisami,[2] admits that while the visible scars of the Pacific War have vanished from Japan, the suffering of the Japanese has not. Indeed, the human condition today may well be worse off than before. While there are signs of prosperity everywhere, the Japanese are "an unhappy, insecure race." They are troubled at heart, lack direction, and have great difficulty in enjoying life.[3]

Understanding the Soka Gakkai's eschatological view of life in Japan is crucial for a full appreciation of what the movement is all about. The theme of the movement is that we live in a world replete with greed and violence and that the Soka Gakkai, together with its parent sect, Nichiren Shoshu, can lead mankind away from the certain destruction of nuclear war to a better and more peaceful world.

Today the Soka Gakkai is a massive religious movement that claims a membership of up to ten percent of the Japanese population and several hundred thousand people abroad, including a half million followers in the United States. Its influence in Japanese society and politics is immense. The Soka Gakkai founded and continues to influence the Komeito, Japan's third ranking political party, which holds approximately ten percent of the seats in the Diet.[4]

The Soka Gakkai is technically the largest of the lay support organizations of the Nichiren Sho sect (Nichiren Shoshu) of Japanese Buddhism. Its tasks are to spread the teaching of the sect to the public, to recruit and support as many members as possible, to involve the membership in as many outside activities as possible, and to protect the sect from outside attack. Nichiren Shoshu derives its theology from its interpretation of the teachings of the thirteenth century Japanese Buddhist monk, Nichiren.

## Eschatology in Japanese Buddhism

Eschatology, the doctrine of last things, is originally a Western concept that refers to Jewish and Christian beliefs concerning the end of the world in its current state, the resurrection of the dead, the Last Judgment, and related matters. The end of this sinful world, the Kingship of God and defeat of evil, the day of judgment, and images of a perfected future are common to both Judaism and Christianity.

Jewish theologians at the time of Christ believed that the Kingdom of God would someday be made manifest on earth. They conceive of this kingdom as having the rule of God on earth, ending life as we know it in this world. The Jews believed that the righteous alone would enter and receive the blessings of the Kingdom of God. The establishment of this realm on earth would involve the punishment of the wicked and the overthrow of heathen political powers under control of God's adversary (ha-satan in Hebrew).

The terms "Kingdom of God" and "Kingdom of Heaven" are frequently used in the New Testament. St. Paul accepted Jesus as the messianic savior who had inaugurated the Kingdom of God and who would soon return on the clouds of heaven to judge the living and the dead. Jesus' "good news" is that the kingdom is at hand and that God accepts sinners and mercifully forgives them.

There is no close parallel to Western eschatology in Buddhism. There is no almighty deity whose rule can destroy evil and bring about a permanent domain of goodness. Neither is there a messianic savior to judge the world. In Japanese Buddhism, however, one can see an eschatological view of life in the concept of mappo. It is eschatological in the sense that the present is viewed as a sinful age and that a better period can exist in the future.

According to the concept of mappo, one may divide the history of the world into three increasingly gloomy periods after Gautama Buddha's entrance into Nirvana: the period of shobo ("true law"), the period of zobo ("imitative law"), and the third period of mappo ("last law" or "latter day of the law").[5] Each of the first two periods endured for about a thousand years. The first period of "true law" is a time when people remembered clearly what the Buddha had taught them and lived by his law. The world was a peaceful and contented place. The second period of "imitative law" is known as a time when there was still general compliance with the Buddha's teachings, but people were drifting away from a strong faith in the Buddha. Although the Buddha's law, or dharma, is still in force during mappo, virtually everybody has forgotten the Buddha's teachings. The result is a time of violence, chaos, and misery. At least a few of the religious leaders of Japan in the thirteenth century believed that they were living at the start of the mappo period.

Medieval scholars of Japanese Buddhism were influenced by such works as the Mappo Tomyo Ki ("Treatise on the Lamp for the Latter Day of the Law"). It is a work traditionally attributed to the Japanese Buddhist philosopher Dengyo, but there are doubts about his authorship. It clarifies the three periods of Buddhist law on the basis of the Kengo (Wise Sutra) and asserts that at the time of its writing, the Middle Day is nearing an end, and in the ensuing Latter Day, Shakyamuni's teachings will remain, but there will be neither practice of his Buddhism nor proof (enlightenment) accruing from it. Furthermore, in the Latter Day there will be no precepts, and even a corrupt monk who does not observe the fundamental teachings of the Buddha might be revered as a great teacher of the people.[6]

During Japan's middle ages, Japan went through radical social change. The relative stability, peace, and glory at the imperial court in Heian-kyo (Kyoto) of the Heian period (785-1185) ended in the fighting of the late twelfth century. The Kamakura era (1185-1333) was an unstable period filled with violence, civil war, and natural disasters that brought a sense of pessimism. Several medieval Buddhist scholars in Japan tried to explain the chaos and depression of their times through the concept of mappo. Such philosophers and religious leaders as Nichiren, Honen, Shinran, and others declared that Japan entered the age of mappo-- according to their calculations--in the year 1052. They felt that individuals could not longer achieve Buddhist enlightenment by their own efforts as had earlier followers of Hinayana Buddhism and even of the Mahayanist sects of Shingon and Tendai esoterifism. There would be no other choice during mappo but for the individual to throw himself on the saving grace of another, such as the Bodhisattva Amida, in the hope of attaining rebirth in paradise.[7]

A great exponent of the idea of mappo was the evangelist Honen (1133-1212). During his career, Honen became increasingly dissatisfied with the older Buddhist methods of seeking enlightenment through individual, merit-producing acts. Instead, he urged total reliance on faith in the saving grace of Amida, whom they considered the only one able to save mankind in this corrupt age.[8] Man was too weak and corrupt to save himself, but if he prayed to Amida by uttering the nembutsu--the calling upon Amida to be saved--he would enter a Pure Land, or paradise, upon death. Mankind was urged to rely upon the saving grace of Amida.

## Nichiren's Eschatological View

Nichiren's life:

The Buddhist leader most affected by the concept of mappo in Japan was Nichiren (1222-82). Nichiren founded the only major sect of Buddhism in Japan that was not derived directly from any sect with ties to China. He was born the son of a poor fisherman in the small fishing village of Kominato on the east coast of Awa Province (present day Chiba prefecture near Tokyo).[9] There is little reliable information about his childhood except for the fact that his parents sent him at age twelve to a Tendai sect temple, Kiyosumidera, some five miles away from his home.[10]

Nichiren remained at Kiyosumidera for four years. His early works show the following: a devotion to esoteric Tendai and Shingon sect teachings, as well as theories of absolute monism derived from Tendai Hongaku (original enlightenment) ideas; a growing faith in the Lotus Sutra,[11] one of the most widely venerated of Mahayana Buddhist scriptures; and a hatred for Pure Land Buddhism.[12]   Later, while living in Kamakura, Nichiren gradually turned away from an esoteric Buddhist faith and moved toward a belief in doctrines.   In so doing he developed an increasingly strong faith in the supremacy of the Lotus Sutra and eternal Buddha Sakyamuni.   It is apparent that Nichiren was also stimulated by the Pure Land belief in the efficacy of the nembutusu, the invocational recitation of the name of the Buddha Amida, as a means of securing birth in Amida's Western Paradise.   Nichiren developed a similar belief in the practice called daimoku (title), a chanting recitation of Namu Mhoho Renge Kyo ("I devote myself to the Mystic Law of the Lotus Sutra"), as an affirmation of the worshiper's belief in the saving powers of the Lotus.   Nichiren insisted that the daimoku of the Lotus contained all of the merits of that sutra and all the virtues of the Buddha.   Those who worshipped the Lotus by chanting the daimoku with complete faith and devotion would receive these merits and virtues.[13]

Nichiren left Kiyosumidera in 1237 to further his education. Nichiren spent ten years studying Tendai at the Tendai temple complex at Mount Hiei near Kyoto and traveling to Kyoto and elsewhere to familiarize himself with the doctrines of other sects. After two decades of study, he returned to his native village in 1253 to proclaim his complete faith in the Lotus Sutra.

Nichiren became a devoted defender of the Lotus Sutra and fervent critic of other Buddhist sects, whose failure to acknowledge the Lotus Nichiren considered blasphemous.  As a result of his open criticism of other sects and his attacks on those government officials supporting these sects, Nichiren was subject to intense government criticism and harassment.  He was arrested on several occasions and spent many of his later years in exile in such remote areas as the island of Sado in the Japan Sea. He died in 1282 at a temple near what is now Tokyo.

Despite his many years in exile, Nichiren remained a prolific student of Buddhism. Among his most famous tracts are Rissho Ankoku Ron ("The Establishment of Righteousness and Security of the Country," 1260), the Kaimokusho ("Opening the Eyes"), and Kanjin no Honzonaho ("The True Object of Worship"). He also wrote many other essays and letters.

Nichiren's Teachings:

After a few years of intensive study at Mount Hiei, Nichiren formulated an apocalyptic view of the deterioration of Japan. The many natural disasters that occurred during his later years, along with the two unsuccessful attempts by Mongol forces to invade Japan in 1274 and 1281, seemed to confirm Nichiren's predictions of internal chaos and foreign invasion.[14]

The apocalyptic view of Nichiren stems from his interpretation of the old Tendai school concept of the Ten Worlds. According to this view, there are at least ten states of mind that dominate a person's world view. All these worlds coexist in a person's mind; however, the dominant state will overshadow the others and will serve as the basis of someone's personality. A person with a dominant "hellish nature" is absorbed with a rage to destroy oneself and everyone else. Too many people like this can bring misery to the state as a whole. A society dominated by strife will see war, destruction, and a breakdown of order.

To combat "the breakdown of order," Nichiren warned against the propagation of false doctrines and stated that the ultimate truth of life lay only in the Lotus Sutra, the basic text of the Greater Vehicle of Buddhism, in which Shakyamuni had revealed that all beings have the potentiality for Buddhahood--that all men

8

can be saved. Nichiren felt that the Tendai Sect, which had based its teachings on the Lotus Sutra when Saicho introduced the sect to Japan early in the ninth century, had strayed from the teachings of the Lotus Sutra and had even spawned new sects, such as those of Pure Land or Amida Buddhism, whose practices differed with those of the Lotus Sutra.[15]

Nichiren accepted the two major points made in the Lotus Sutra. The first is that the Buddha was not just a man, but a manifestation of an eternal, all-pervading Buddha-nature. Shakyamuni was only one of an endless series of buddhas who are born into the world of man, who go through the process of becoming enlightened to demonstrate the experience of mankind, and who, upon death, enter a state of nirvana from which there is no reincarnation. The second concept is that of a buddha-nature, or life force, that is universal and all-pervading and which exists in all beings. Thus, buddha-nature exists in all of us all the time and forms the very core of our being; even during mappo we can all attain Buddhahood.[16]

Having concluded that the Lotus Sutra offered man the only real chance for salvation during mappo, Nichiren wrote that "the Lotus represents the true teaching of the Buddha. Buddha himself realized that ... with the coming of mappo, this sutra must be spread to the rest of the world to save humanity."[17]  Nichiren concluded that the Lotus Sutra had been expounded for the sake of sinners living at the start of the mappo period and that a strong effort must be made to introduce the Lotus to the rest of humanity.

Nichiren believed that the Lotus was the one vehicle that could provide mankind with an escape from agony of mappo to a new era of eternal peace and happiness. He was sure that nobody else had understood the "true" doctrines of the Lotus, so he felt he had an absolute obligation to spread its teachings to his fellow man. He was convinced that if all mankind joined him in worshipping the Lotus, the natural disasters facing Japan and the individual hardships facing the Japanese would disappear. Today, Nichiren groups, such as Nichiren Soshu and the Soka Gakkai, have accepted their master's view of mappo and see his teachings as the only way to lead mankind out of its present quagmire. Nichiren summed up his mission as follows:

> I have appeared in Japan in this time of emergency by the order of the Buddha. I dare say that I am not fortunate. However, the order of the King of the Law is categorical. Therefore, according to the Lotus Sutra, I raise the army of the true teaching against the forces of provisional teachings, wear the armor of patience, take the sword of the wonderful Law, bend the bow of the Revelation of the Truth, fix the arrow of honesty, ride in the white bullock-cart of equality, break the gate of provisional teachings, and hurl criticism at the followers of the Nembutsu, Shingon, Zen, Ritsu and other sects. Some of them run away or withdraw, while others are captured and become my disciples. I will repeat the offensive. I will march on, although they are many and my friends are few.[18]

The goal of Nichiren's Buddhism, therefore, is to move as many people as possible from the misery of a hellish mind to the peaceful, joyful, and understanding state of Buddhahood. Buddhahood is not something you attain at death; any person can achieve it here and not without proper faith in the teachings of the Lotus Sutra and the propagation of these doctrines to others. According to Nichiren, Shakyamuni promises to bring enlightenment and true happiness to all those who have profound faith in his teachings and invoke any part of the Lotus Sutra as a sign of their faith.[19] Nichiren believed the Lotus to have the power of saving all people and that it was especially designed for a period when the world was dominated by evil. Nichiren wrote that "the

Lotus represents the true teaching of the Buddha. Buddha himself realized that...with the coming of mappo, this sutra must be spread to the rest of the world to save humanity."[20] The Lotus is indeed "expounded for the sake of us sinful men living at the beginning of mappo,"[21] and an all-out effort must be made to introduce the Lotus to the rest of humanity.

Rissho Ankokuy Ron:

Nichiren wrote Rissho Ankoku Ron (RAR) in 1260 when Japan was experiencing a large number of natural disasters, was suffering from domestic wars, and was facing the possibility of a Mongolian invasion. Nichiren wrote RAR to convince the shogunate that the cause of the nation's despair stemmed from a religious base--the failure of the people to follow the true teachings of the Buddha, and the shogunate's willingness to give alms to priests from other "false sects."[22] (Several of the sutras that Nichiren had studied were known as "nation-protecting sutras" [chingo kokka kho] which promised the protection of various gods to the country that reveres the sutra.[23]

Nichiren tried to find the cause of the national calamities and social unrest in Japan and came to the conclusion that a stable, peaceful society could exist only if the correct Buddhist teachings had been accepted by the people.[24] Nichiren felt that redemption could be gained only here and now in this world. The sentient world could become a Buddhist paradise if people would turn to the correct from of Buddhism.[25]

As a means of bringing these thoughts to the attention of the bakufu (shogunate), Nichiren wrote Rissho Ankoku Ron as a treatise to the most powerful person in the government, Hojo Tokiyori. In the treatise, Nichiren contends that Japan's secular leaders, especially high government leaders, have brought misery to the people because of their support or tolerance of "false" religious sects. Nichiren states that these officials should withdraw their support from these sects and give Nichiren and his followers a free hand to propagate the only religious doctrines that would bring peace and happiness to the land.

Nichiren wrote RAR in the form of a dialogue between an intelligent Buddhist priest, who is Nichiren himself, and a guest who asks many leading and provocative questions, which Nichiren answers in detail. The guest sets the tone for the whole treatise by noting at the outset:

> During recent years cosmic cataclysms, natural disasters, famines, and epidemics have filled the world. Oxen and horses collapse at the crossroads, skeletons fill the lanes. Already more than half the population has died; no one is free from affliction.... (People invoke Amida's name and others pray to a variety of deities.) But while we rack our minds and bodies, famine and plague grow more menacing. Everywhere we see beggars; our eyes cannot escape the sight of death.... Why then is the world crumbling so fast and the Buddha Law decaying...[26]

Nichiren replies that people have forgotten the Buddha's teachings:

> They turn their backs on the Truth and return to evil ways. For this reason the (guardian) gods have left the country; and the sages have departed. The evil spirits and demons rush in; troubles arrive, and calamities spring up...[27]

Quoting from scripture, Nichiren states:

> (When) the saints will abandon the country..., the seven calamities will occur...there will be: pestilence among the people, foreign invasion, civil revolt, stars wandering from their heavenly positions, eclipses of the sun and moon, typhoons out of season, prolonged drought.[28]

In RAR, Nichiren reserves his harshest attacks not against political leaders, but against other religious sects, especially the Amidists. Nichiren concludes that these practitioners of false religions have led the people and government away from the true teachings and powers of the Lotus Sutra. His solution is easy: "If we hurry to stop alms to heretics and give alms instead to monks and nuns of the true faith, if we cleanse the kingdom of these bandits," society will be transformed into a Buddhist utopia.[29]

At the end of RAR, Nichiren gives one an idea of what his Buddhist world paradise will be like. It will be a realm which does not suffer from the seven calamities and which is guarded by good gods. The country will be safe and peaceful, there will be no natural disasters, crops will be bountiful, and all the people will live together in great happiness and harmony, assured of peace in their present and future lives:

> The time will come when all people, including those of Learning, Realization, and Bodhisattva, will enter on the path of Buddhahood, and the Mystic Law alone will flourish throughout the land. In that time, because all people chant Nam-Myoho-Renge-Kyo together, the wind will not beleaguer the branches or boughs, nor will the rain fall hard enough to break a clod. The world will become as it was in the ages of Fu Shi and Shn Nung[30] in ancient China. Disasters will be driven from the land, and the people will be rid of misfortune. They will also learn the art of living long, fulfilling lives...[31]

Nichiren's eschatological view of world history thus has a bright future. In his tract Kaimokusho, Nichiren states that at the darkest and most desperate time during mappo, followers of the Lotus Sutra will preach the ultimate truth of the Lotus Sutra. Gradually people will come to see the value of the Lotus Sutra and will pray to it with full faith. Thus, the Lotus, and the daimoku, the symbol of the entire strength and truth of the Lotus Sutra itself, will become the object of worship. Those chanting the daimoku will gradually attain better karma and enter a higher realm of the Ten Worlds. When all mankind abandons other false or lesser teachings and practices the chanting of the daimoku, all of humanity will eventually achieve Buddhahood in this lifetime.

Nichiren Shoshu

Nichiren Shoshu, the parent sect of the Soka Gakkai, is one of several Nichiren sects that trace their origins back to Nichiren himself and that comprise the Nichiren school of Buddhism in Japan today. Some of Nichiren Shoshu's teachings and eschatological views, however, differ sharply from those held by some of the other Nichiren sects.

While most Nichiren sects regard the Buddha Shakyamuni has the true eternal Buddha, Nichiren Shoshu insists that Nichiren himself is the "True Budda of the age of mappo."[32] It insists that Shakyamuni is a presursor who lit the way for the true Buddha, who would come during the darkest period of mappo to lead mankind to enlightenment and salvation. Since Nichiren was born during mappo and brought the saving powers of the Lotus Sutra to the attention of mankind, he must be the true Buddha. Shakyamuni's prescriptions for salvation were difficult to follow and only comprehensible to a few individuals, but Nichiren offered a very simple formula--the chanting of the daimoku--so very simple and yet so powerful that any person with faith could utter that simple formula (Namu-Myoho-Renge-Kyo) and achieve Buddhahood in this lifetime. Thus, Nichiren and his followers are the only ones capable of leading mankind to salvation. Nichiren Shoshu refers to its patron as Nichiren Daishonin.[33]

Another crucial distinction between Nichiren Shoshu and other Nichiren sects concerns the status of a mandala[34] which

Nichiren Shoshu claims that Nichiren constructed shortly before his death. A common feature of many Nichiren Shoshu temples in Japan is a mandala, which is revered as a central object of worship. These mandalas were either inscribed by Nichiren himself or are copies of originals and are displayed on an altar or in some prominent part of the temple. They are roughly one-and-a-half meters high, about half a meter wide, and slightly less than ten centimeters thick. The seven kanji (Chinese characters) of the daimoku are usually written prominently down the middle.

Soka Gakkai officials claim that of the roughly 130 mandalas prepared by Nichiren, the significant one was composed on the twelfth day of the tenth month of 1279. The other mandalas are not without value, but only the 1279 mandala is regarded as being efficacious for the salvation of mankind. It is called the Daigohonzon[35] to distinguish it form replicas, known as gohonzon, found in Nichiren Shoshu temples and members' homes. It is said that Nichiren's main purpose for coming to earth was to inscribe this Daigohonzon.[36] Other Nichiren sects dispute the notion that Nichiren is the "True Buddha" and that there is any special significance attached to the 1279 gohonzon. Nichiren Shoshu and Soka Gakkai officials contend that the gohonzon now enshrined in the Sho Hondo (Main Hall of Worship) at Taiseki-ji, the head temple of Nichiren Shoshu located directly under Mount Fuji in Shizuoka Prefecture, is the one Nichiren composed in 1279 for the salvation of mankind.

Nichiren Shoshu claims that the Daigohonzon is the embodiment of Nichiren, the Buddha, and of the law of the universe, the daimoku. It is said that though Nichiren was a mortal who died in 1282, he continues to live through the gohonzon, which embodies him and his doctrines. The Daigohonzon is said also to symbolize the universe as a whole and the basic laws of life; consequently, it represents the daimoku, the fundamental law of existence. The only path to salvation is the chanting the seven syllables of the daimoku before the Daigohonzon or an authorized replica.

Thus, the Soka Gakkai's and Nichiren Shoshu's solution to the eschatological problem facing mankind is really quite simple: Man will not find salvation or enlightenment in another realm after death; instead, he can attain Buddhahood[37] here and now. According to the Tendai theory of Ten Worlds, there are ten states of mind that are always present in the personality of every human. Every human is dominated by one of these ten psychological states, which range from Hell[38] to Buddhahood.[39]

Evil exists in the world today because mankind is dominated by hellish natures. Men hate each other and nations go to war because of the brutal natures of people living in this hell. The cause of man's sad state is bad karma.[40] The key to a better life is changing one's karma. A better karma will lead one to a higher "world." A perfectly clean or pure karma allows one to become a Buddha, a kind and loving person whose wisdom and devotion to others makes him a superior human.

Nichiren Shoshu and the Soka Gakkai claim that mankind can gain redemption and achieve Buddhahood by changing the nature of its karma. If mankind as a whole had a good karma, then men would love each other, greed and violence would quickly disappear, war would become a thing of the past, and nations would live in peace. The reality of the present is that mankind, with its hellish nature, is heading down the path toward nuclear war, one realization of hell in this world. Nichiren Shoshu and the Soka Gakkai offer their religion as the only sure way to protect mankind from his own hell. Their eschatological view of the world envisions a bright and beautiful tomorrow where people will direct their creative energies toward peace and mutual respect rather than war.

According to Nichiren Shoshu and the Soka Gakkai, the collective karma of a nation or of mankind as a whole will only change with the massive change of individual karmas. The change of a person's karma from a depraved to a more blessed state is termed the "Human Revolution" (ningen kakumei). The proselytization of the faith and its acceptance by others is kosen rufu, which literally means "widely declare and spread Buddhism."

Nichiren Shosu and the Soka Gakkai believe that they alone can save mankind because of their beliefs that Nichiren is the true Buddha for the age of mappo and that the Daigohonzon, which alone has the power to save mankind, is housed in their head temple at Taisekiji. Thus, if man is to be saved, he must convert to Nichiren Shoshu and worship the Daigohonzon by chanting the daimoku before it or a recognized replica. If enough people do this, the negative karma of society will disappear, the hellish world of mappo will come to an end, and we will live in a beautiful and peaceful Buddhaland.

# NOTES

[1]The movie <u>Ningen Kakumei</u> (1976) is the film version of a series of books of the same title written by Ikeda Daisaku, the third president of the Soka Gakkai. The books present a semi-fictional account of the Soka Gakkai's history from the 1930s through the death of the Soka Gakkai's second president, Toda Josei, in 1958.

[2]All Japanese names are presented here in the traditional Japanese order with last names preceding the given name.

[3]Interview with Yamazaki Hisami in Tokyo, 1 August 1984.

[4]The Soka Gakkai founded the Komeito in 1964 and had direct control over the party until 1970 when it officially severed its ties with the party. Despite this official break, however, the Soka Gakkai's emotional ties with and influence on the Komeito are significant. A vast majority of Komeito candidates and voters are Gakkai members.

[5]Skt. <u>Saddharma - vioralpopa</u>.

[6]Nichiren Shoshu International Center, <u>A Dictionary of Buddhist Terms and Concepts</u> (Tokyo, 1983), p. 258.

[7]H. Paul Varley, <u>Japanese Culture: A Short Story</u> (New York, 1977), p. 51.

[8]Ibid., p. 69.

[9]On Tatsunosuke, <u>Nichiren</u> (Tokyo, 1974), p. 1.

[10]Imai Masaharu and Nakao Takashi, <u>Nihon Meiso Jiten</u> (Tokyo, 1976), p. 147.

[11]Skt: <u>Saddharmapundarika-sutra</u>; Japanese: <u>Myohorenge-kyo</u> or <u>Hokkekyo</u>.

[12]H.G. Lamont, "Nichiren," in <u>The Encyclopedia of Japan</u>, Vol. V (Tokyo, 1983), p. 375.

[13]Ibid.

[14]Varley, pp. 71-72.

[15]Ibid.

[16]Laurel R. Rodd, Nichiren: Selected Writings (Honolulu, 1980), pp. 34-35.

[17]Ibid.

[18]Quoted in Hoshino Eizen and Murano Senchu, The Lotus Sutra and Nichiren (Jimokuji, Aichi Prefecture, 1968), p. 8.

[19]Murano Senchu, trans., The Lotus Sutra (Tokyo, 1974), pp. 43-44.

[20]Murano Senchu, trans. Nichiren Nhorai Metsugo Gohyakusai Shi Kanjin Honzonsho or The True Object of Worship Revealed for the First Time in the Fifth of Five Century Periods After the Great Decease of the Tathagata (Tokyo, 1954), p. 37.

[21]Quoted in R. C. Armstrong, An Introduction to Japanese Buddhism (New York, 1952), p. 239.

[22]Tamura Yoshiro, Nichiren: Selected Writings (Honolulu, 1980), p. 8.

[23]Rodd, p. 9.

[24]Tamura, pp. 60-64.

[25]Rodd, p. 10.

[26]Ibid., pp. 59-60.

[27]Ibid., p. 60.

[28]Ibid., p. 62.

[29]Ibid., p. 74.

[30]Fu Shi and Shen Nung: Legendary kings who reigned over ideal societies in ancient China. Their reigns embodied the Confucian concept of Utopia.

[31]Nichiren Shoshu International Center, Major Writings of Nichiren Daishonin (Tokyo, 1979), Vol. 1, pp. 101-2.

[32]Nichiren declared that the true object of worship of his faith must be the Buddha, Shakyamuni, who announced his eternity in the 16th chapter of the

Lotus. There are three distinct yet interrelated and unified aspects of this supreme being, namely, the eternal Buddha, the Law and the envoy who would spread the Buddha's teachings. Nichiren's followers today dispute the actual make-up of these three Treasures, but Nichiren himself clarified his stand as follows.

Shakyamuni is the only true Buddha; he is omnipotent, eternal and the mighty savior of mankind. He came to earth in the guise of a human being to realize his vow to save mankind, but he is in fact far greater than any other being. The treasure of the Law is the Lotus Sutra, which is the highest teaching of and the actual embodiment of the Buddha. The Law is symbolized in five characters of the Daimoku. Jogyo is the sacred envoy who is obliged to spread the Buddha's teachings throughout the universe, and Nichiren may have seen himself as the reincarnation of this Bodhisattva who is found in the Sutra.

See: Nakagawa Nisshi, Nichirenshugi no Joshiki (Kyoto, 1970), pp. 46-48 and 51-68.

[33]Daishon is equivalent to "very holy one" or "saint."

[34]In Esoteric Buddhism a mandala is a "diagrammic picture which represents the cosmic nature of the Buddhas, Bodhissatvas, and other divine beings. It is regarded as a symbol of the universe and is used as an aid in meditation." Japanese-English Buddhist Dictionary (Tokyo, 1965), p. 124.

[35]In Japanese an object of worship is called a honzon, which means "object of fundamental respect." Go is an honorific prefix. Dai is a prefix which means "great."

[36]Toda Josei, Lecture on the Sutra (Tokyo, 1968), pp. 3-5.

[37]The term "Buddha" means one who has attained wisdom or enlightenment. Buddhahood is the state of being of one who has become enlightened. Any human who attains this state can become a Buddha.

[38]A hellish nature; a condition in which one is dominated by the impulse of rage to destroy oneself and everything else. People with these conditions are warlike and violent. They attack others with no apparent reason. The Soka Gakkai, for example, states that Germany was dominated by people with hellish natures during the Nazi era and that this was the reason that Germany was responsible for so much evil two generations ago.

[39]"This is a condition of perfect and absolute freedom, in which one enjoys boundless wisdom and compassion, and is filled with the courage and power to surmount all hardships. A Buddha understands all phenomena and realizes the Middle Way." The Nichiren Shoshu International Center, A Dictionary of Buddhist Terms and Concepts (Tokyo, 1983), p. 444.

20

[40]Karma is a Buddhist doctrine that one's state in life is a result of actions (physical and mental) in past incarnations and that action in this life can determine one's destiny in future lives. Karma is a natural, impersonal, moral law of cause and effect.

# CHAPTER 2

## TODA JOSEI AND THE REVIVAL OF THE SOKA GAKKAI
## AFTER WORLD WAR II

During the closing months of World War II, the eschatological views of the Soka Gakkai originated in the mind of Toda Josei (1900-1958), the second president of the Soka Gakkai and its true founder. Spending a considerable period of time in prison during the war, Toda suffered greatly. He was depressed not only by his imprisonment, but also by the collapse of his publishing empire and the horrendous destruction of Japan. Suddenly he saw hope for a new life for himself, Japan, and the world through the doctrines of Nichiren Shoshu. Thus, the modern Soka Gakkai was born among the ashes and depression of a defeated Japan.

The American occupation of Japan (1945-52) saw such an explosion of newly formed religions that the period is often referred to as the "Rush Hour of the Gods." Of the 207 registered religious organizations in 1947, 136 were called "New Religions" because they had no traditional ties with Japan's more traditional religions.[1] A few of these New Religions had prewar roots, but those that prospered after the war grew as a result of the unique conditions of the Occupation period. Three important reasons for their success are: (1) the spread of religious freedom; (2) the dismal failure of government policies and ideologies during World War II; (3) the poverty, desperation, and loneliness of many Japanese during this period.[2] In many cases these religious organizations attracted a mass following numbering in the tens of thousands. The Soka Gakkai experienced its real birth during this period.

Eric Hoffer, in an essay on mass movements, wrote: "A movement is pioneered by men of words, materialized by fanatics, and consolidated by men of action."[3] H. Neill McFarland in his book, The Rush Hour of the Gods, wrote:

> Though Soka Gakkai was not among his (Hoffer's) referents, it fits quite neatly the pattern that he described... Its (first) three presidents typify respectively these three categories. The first president, Makiguchi Tsunesaburo (1871-1944), was the man of words who founded the society. Toda Josei (1900-1958), the second president, was the fanatic, under whose leadership the organization achieved its most spectacular growth. The man of action is the third president, Ikeda Daisaku (1928- ), who is succeeding in making more and more observers acknowledge that the Soka Gakkai is more than an emotion. It is a monumental reality.[4]

This is the popular conception of the Soka Gakkai's history, but it is not an entirely correct perception. While it is true that Makiguchi created the society in the 1930s and made the essential connection between it and the Nichiren Sho sect, it was Toda who reestablished the group after World War II and gave it its present character and direction. There was no view of eschatology in the prewar Soka Gakkai. Toda's principal role was that of organizer. He was also a man of words whose lectures, books, and articles gave the Soka Gakkai much of its present philosophical foundation based on eschatology. The real foundation period of the Soka Gakkai is not the 1930s, but 1943-51. Between the years 1943-45, Toda, while in prison, redefined his religious ideas and decided to devote his life to the spread of these ideas. From 1945-51, Toda reconstructed the Soka Gakkai to conform to his own beliefs.

A brief analysis of the ideology and goals of the prewar Soka Kyoiku Gakkai and those of its postwar successor will show notable differences in terms of direction, emphasis, and goals.

Makiguchi was primarily interested in educational reform, while Toda wanted to reform the human spirit and to lead man from certain doom to a better way of life. Other than the continued involvement of some people and superficial similarities in doctrine, there is very little that they have in common. Thus, it is not correct to include the Soka Gakkai among the prewar New Religions. Rather, the Soka Gakkai is a movement that grew up in the aftermath of war and was led by a man who saw acute misery and who felt that he had a solution to the problems.

## The Soka Kyoiku Gakkai

The Soka Gakkai states that it was founded in 1930 when Makiguchi retired from his career as a teacher and school administrator and began publishing his magnum opus, Soka Kyoiku-gaku Taikei ("A system of Value-Creation Education").[5] The society was not formally organized until 1937, however, when about sixty educators formed the Soka Kyoiku Gakkai (Value Creating Educational Society) with Makiguchi as its president.[6] The society was organized to promote Makiguchi's educational ideas. Until 1937 Makiguchi's concerns were secular--he was primarily interested in educational reform. After 1937, however, Makiguchi's concerns became increasingly religious.[7]

The Soka Kyoiku Gakkai's doctrines were based on Makiguchi's Philosophy of Value (kachiron), or value creation, which he regarded as the most important element of human life. Makiguchi wrote that while the values of individuals may differ, mankind shares a common search for an improvement of his lot:

> The highest and ultimate object of life is happiness (kofuku), and the goal of life is none but the attainment and creation of value which is in itself happiness. Happiness is a state of man's life--an ideal state for which everyone thirsts whether or not

he is aware of it. It has innumerbale stages, with unhappiness at one antipode, but man lives to attain the highest stage of happiness...a happy life signifies none other than the state of existence in which one can gain and create value in full.[8]

Makiguchi stated that Western philosophers such as Kant suggest that the ultimate values of life should be truth, good, and beauty. Makiguchi challenged this view by contending that gain should be substituted for truth; and man achieve happiness through a search for beauty, (bi), gain (ri), and good (zen).[9] Since man's life is dominated by a desire to improve his lot, he seeks to acquire or create new things to meet his diverse demands.

A key point of this system of values is the premise that truth, traditionally the primary value, is in fact not a value. To Makiguchi, truth and value are concepts on entirely different plains. Makiguchi defined truth as a "concept which objectifies the relationship between a being such as man and something in this environment." Value, on the other hand, is noted as a subjective relationship between the two--a man and the thing.[10]

The point of education, according to Makiguchi, is to teach man how to create value. A piece of wood in itself has no value to a man, but if he cuts it into pieces and nails them together in a certain way, he can build a home which has both intrinsic and real value. Makiguchi was critical of Japan's educational system because it stressed rote memorization--how could a person learn to cope in a complex world if all he learned was a few pat formulas? Makiguchi suggested that students spend half the school day in class and the other half working in the community.

The purpose of Makiguchi's educational program was to teach people how to "acquire competence as creators of value and thus find happiness."[11] Since personal and social happiness are the basic aims of mankind, man must learn how to find a workable balance between individual and social values. A person must realize his responsibilities to society and be able to make personal decisions which can help him without hurting society. Consequently, an educational system that concentrates only on the teaching of truth can in no way prepare a person for his most important task in life, the creation of value.

Makiguchi contended that among the three elements of value, beauty and gain pertain to the individual, while good is a social value. He also emphasized that one must include such negative values as ugliness, loss, and evil to form a meaningful contrast to the positive values. A person must strive not only to avoid these negative values, but also to improve himself while seeking to improve the overall value of society.

Makiguchi stressed that people need the skills of cognition and evaluation. Japanese schools emphasized cognition--the fact that $1+1=2$. This emphasis is based on an empirical view of the world, through which one learns to discern the meaning of a new perception based on past experience. Makiguchi pointed out that man does not have a priori abilities. Evaluation, in contrast, involves a critical view, which is reflected in such a statement as "A cat is beautiful." Hence, cognition is related to truth while value is based on evaluation.[12]

Makiguchi emphasized that both cognition and evaluation are necessary for a basic understanding of the external world and that understanding would be incomplete without the inclusion of both. He inferred that value judgments are extremely personal and must not be accepted as truth by others. Unfortunately, so many people accept an evaluation as the truth that they are confused and stalled in their efforts to create value.[13]

In summary, Makiguchi proposed a utilitarian explanation of society, which he hoped mankind would use to find real happiness. Man is the master of his own destiny, and he must learn how to manipulate his natural and social environment in an appropriate manner to better his standing in life. Through past experience he must learn to distinguish between that which is bad or good for him and to proceed toward the good. He must work hard to achieve lasting happiness in life both for himself and for society as a whole, and he must learn to maximize his own values without inflicting harm on others. There is no hint of the eschatology of Toda in the writings of Makiguchi.

Makiguchi stressed that man is unhappy because he does not know how to maximize positive values.[14] To correct this situation, Makiguchi suggested that man study his relationship with his environment with the greatest of care so that he may learn how to live a productive and meaningful life within the confines of society. Personal freedom and the right to seek one's own path in life are absolute necessities in life, since man cannot be happy unless he can adopt a lifestyle that suits him. However, the individual must accept the basic rules of society and make a true effort to make his nation or community a better place in which to live, since one cannot be happy in a society that is basically bad.

Makiguchi and Toda, his trusted lieutenant, were converted to the Nichiren Sho sect in 1928, but it is uncertain how deep their religious commitment was during the following decade. It is clear, however, that by the late 1930s Makiguchi and Toda began to develop more interest in religion at a time when Makiguchi's educational ideas were winning very few converts. Perhaps Makiguchi became more involved with religion as a result of his depression over the failure of his educational mission. Nevertheless, he became increasingly active in Nichiren Shoshu activities and on occasion wrote or spoke on religious matters. It is apparent that the shift away from an educational emphasis to a more religious orientation began after 1937, and it is interesting to note that there was a shift in membership away from educators towards people primarily interested in religion.[15]

Religion, according to Makiguchi, is the "fundamental teaching which regulates individual life."[16] It gives man the criteria to judge the values of beauty, gain, and good. Religion should also be the "thing which serves as the fundamental principle and indispensable standard for bringing happiness in the real sense and for establishing a peaceful and happy world."[17] The main task then is to find a religion which can bring the most happiness to the lives of men.

Makiguchi concluded that only the Buddhism of Nichiren as taught by Nichiren Shoshu can bring true happiness to the individual and peace to society. It saves the individual by giving him the maximum gain and saves society by establishing the highest good. According to Makiguchi, the Japanese monk Nichiren (1222-82) taught man the true way to salvation by invoking the daimoku before a gohonzon. No other religion can possibly lead one to salvation. Through the "true" Buddhism of Nichiren, one will obtain the maximum amount of happiness, since personal gain and beauty will be acquired to the maximum extent, and people will make positive contributions to society to achieve social good. Consequently, if one firmly believes in the power of the gohonzon and chants the daimoku while facing it, "his prayer will be answered, he can acquire vital life force, and a peaceful society is established."[18] Man can acquire the maximum individual and societal contact through faith in the gohonzon.

Between 1937 and 1943, the Soka Kyoiku Gakkai (SKG) grew to about three thousand members with its headquarters in Tokyo and several small branches across the country. At regularly held meetings, members reported the results of their educational research and personal experiences. In addition, the Soka Kyoiku Gakkai published a journal (<u>Kachi Sozo</u>: "Creation of Value").[19]

World War II endangered the independence of the Soka Kyoiku Gakkai. At the start of the Pacific War, the Japanese government intensified its efforts to merge various Buddhist sects in the cause of national unity. The 1940 Religious Organizations Law gave the state control over religions and allowed it to use religions to enhance the war effort. Although there was a strong effort to unify all the Nichiren sects, many lay and clerical followers of Nichiren Shoshu decided against a merger because Nichiren had taught his followers that they should avoid all involvement with other "false" sects and with the government--that independence must be maintained. Nichiren Shoshu, perhaps because of its small size and the remoteness then of its main temple, Taiseki-ji, was allowed to maintain its independence.

Makiguchi nevertheless spoke out against the government's religious policies. Adopting a stance similar to that of Nichiren when he wrote his treatise <u>Rissho Ankoku Ron</u>, Makiguchi ardently maintained that Japan would prosper once the state recognized Nichiren Shoshu, the "only correct religion." By 1942 the government began surveillance of the group, banned its publications, and ordered a stop to proselytizing. When Makiguchi and others disobeyed these orders, the government arrested them in July, 1943. Other members renounced their faith and were released, but Toda and Makiguchi refused to do so. They remained in prison. Sadly, Makiguchi died in prison of old age and malnutrition on November 18, 1944. Toda remained there until his release on bail on July 3, 1945, only a few weeks before the dramatic end of the war.

One Soka Gakkai scholar, Suematsu Yoshinori, argues that Makiguchi was primarily interested in changing society as a whole-in bringing about a revolution that would rid society of unhappiness and militarism.[20] According to Suematsu, Makiguchi saw education as the key to revolution; if one could change Japan's youth through education, these children would grow up and bring dramatic change to society as a whole. Suematsu argues that it was only later that Makiguchi found solace through religion and came to the conclusion that deeper, more meaningful change could come from the religious conversion of the people to Nichiren Shoshu which would bring immediate benefits to all converts. The result would be the peaceful and happy society as described by Nichiren and Rissho Ankoku Ron.[21]

Suematsu also depicts Makiguchi as a martyr who was deeply opposed to the militarism of Japan and the war effort; however, the facts do not necessarily support this. Makiguchi only turned against the government when it tried to merge Nichiren Shoshu with other Buddhist sects. He was a man of great courage and conviction, but not the militant pacifist praised by some Gakkai members today.

There is little written evidence to support Suematsu's assertion that Makiguchi made the full switch away from a movement based on education--a secular concern--to one based strictly on religion. Although religion was becoming increasingly important to Makiguchi and his followers, the small movement was still anchored to the educational aims of its founder. The old SKG died with Makiguchi. It was Toda who removed education and "value creation" from center stage and who launched the Soka Gakkai as a strictly religious movement that only much later would develop an interest in such things as education.

## Birth of the Soka Gakkai

The Soka Gakkai which grew up under the aegis of Toda Josei had a very different focus from the SKG and grew for entirely different reasons. In today's Soka Gakkai, Makiguchi is treated as a remote ancestor, and there is little mention of his work. Although little is said about it openly, toda is treated as the real founder. It is also clear that Toda's postwar activities grew out of an intense religious experience that occurred as he sat in lonely isolation in a small dark cell for nearly two years.

Toda claims that he attained enlightenment in prison only after he had chanted the daimoku two million times and had read the Lotus Sutra with great care. He later emphasized that chanting the daimoku so often was a crucial element in his efforts because it fused his life with that of the universe and allowed him to discover the nature of life itself. Toda felt that study alone would never help anyone achieve enlightenment and that religious practice, together with some study, is the key to salvation. Practice implies strong faith, and Nichiren Buddhism puts a very heavy emphasis on faith.[22]

While in prison, Toda read the sixteenth chapter of the Lotus Sutra in which Shakyamuni revealed his eternal existence and the all-pervasiveness of his spirit. But Toda did not understand what Shakyamuni meant by "eternal life." What role, he wondered was the Buddha supposed to play in the Lotus? What is meant by "Buddha-nature?" Most importantly, Toda wondered about the nature of life itself. Does life end with death?[23]

While reading part of the Lotus, Toda came on the following passage starting that the Buddha's body is the following:

> Neither existing nor nonexisting; without cause or condition, without self or others; neither square nor round, neither short nor long; without appearance or

disappearance; without birth or death; neither created or emanating, neither made or produced; neither sitting or lying; neither walking or stopping; neither moving or rolling; neither right nor wrong; without merit or demerit; neither that or this; neither going nor coming; neither blue nor yellow; neither red nor white; neither crimson nor purple, without a variety of color.[24]

Toda wondered what the Buddha could be if he were none of the above. After much thought, Toda came up with an inspiration. Two words flashed in his mind--life force! Life force is "neither existing nor non-existing; without cause or condition; without self..." The Buddha is the very essence of the cosmic life force, which is basic to everything and thus has no definable existence. This explains all the negatives describing the Buddha in the Lotus. Life force is not subject to time limits and pervades all things in the three stages of existence--past, present, and future.[25]

Toda's personal discovery that the true substance of Buddhahood is a cosmic life force that forms the basis of the lives of human beings is the basis of his enlightenment. This discovery permitted him to find what he felt was the hidden meaning of the Lotus Sutra. Further study of the Lotus Sutra convinced Toda that the Buddha was trying to tell mankind that the Buddha-nature in us is of immense beauty and is available to all men if only they could find it--that they only have to know HOW to search for the truth.

Toda described his revelation in his essay, Seimeiron ("Dialogue on Life") which consists of four parts. In the second part, Toda declares that life is eternal; it has existed in the past, is here now, and will always be here. It has no limits in time or space and dominates and permeates everything. Buddhism, in other words, is the explanation of life itself. Man can explain every aspect of life through Buddhism, including the causes of human suffering. Life is governed by the laws of cause and effect. Man, however, can only find liberation through the truths revealed in the Lotus Sutra and through the key teachings of Nichiren. Therefore, it is through the Buddhism of Nichiren that many may find release from the pain and suffering of life.

> Life exists together with the universe; it did not precede the universe, it did not come into existence accidently and it is not created by some being. The universe is itself life and it is an error to say that life is merely a monopoly of this planet alone. We (members of the Soka Gakkai) are trying to grasp the true nature of sacred life through the infinite mercy of Nichiren and through our belief in the Daigohonzon, which is the true embodiment of salvation and enlightenment...[26]

> Consider the nature of the universe. It is in a continuous state of flux. Nothing remains the same. From the immense rolling and swirling of countless galaxies to our own small solar system, an immutable universal law governs everything....We too (are) part of something infinite. That something is life force, which Nichiren Daishonin distilled into the Mystic or Supreme Law of Nam-myoho-renge-kyo and then gave physical embodiment in the Daigohonzon. This marvelous life force operates throughout the entire universe, in the most distant stars and in the life of each individual being. This is the basic truth on which everything rests. Without knowledge of this truth, faith is impossible. But with faith arising from the knowledge of the nature of all life, we have power to work changes in karma, the law of cause and effect that governs everything in the universe.[27]

It is said that as a result of these revelations in prison, an "extremely strange sensation" seized Toda, and "a world which I could never see before unfolded itself in front of me." His body quaking with ecstatic joy, Toda stood in his cell and shouted to "All Buddhas, all Bodhisattvas, and all common men of the world" that he had now found, at the age of forty-five, "the true meaning of life."[28]

This episode marks the true start of the New Soka Gakkai. The whole Soka Gakkai movement today revolves around Toda's discovery. Today there is little talk of "value creation" as expressed by Makiguchi. Rather, the emphasis is on the role that the daimoku and Daigohonzon play in the salvation of individuals and how the gradual spread of individual salvation will lead to universal happiness.

It is said that when Toda was released on July 3, 1945, he left jail weakened physically but greatly strengthened spiritually. Toda was "burning with a desire for vengeance--not against the militarist government of Japan, but against an invisible enemy who had caused his own suffering of more than two years as well as his teacher's death in jail and agony to tens of millions of his fellow countrymen."[29]

At this time Toda remembered Nichiren's statement in Rissho Ankoku Ron that when a nation follows false religions and persecutes the true Buddhism, it becomes filled with heresy. "At such a time the Buddha will send the guardian deities Bonten and Taishaku to mete out punishment. It suddenly became quite clear to Toda that MacArthur corresponded to Bonten in his role of judge of those who ignored the true faith and led Japan to destruction."[30] MacArthur's task was to make structural reforms in order to remove the corrupt militarists who had imprisoned Toda and who had led the nation to ruin. These structural reforms would create a democratic environment in which Toda and his followers could work without outside interference. Toda's task was to liberate the nation by establishing the true Buddhism of Nichiren.

MacArthur's directive guaranteeing the freedom of religions was warmly received by Toda:

Not a Japanese, but a foreign conqueror had affected this reform. It was indeed the work of Bonten, as prophesied in the Gosho (Nichiren's complete works). No longer could the government hinder religious activities; the Japanese people would be saved.

Although Toda had never met the great soldier (MacArthur), he had accurately assessed his role as the new ruler of Japan. It was tragic that Japan had been defeated and was now occupied by foreigners, but it is even more tragic when the minds of a whole people are dominated by hatred, anger and animality and when nations and societies are ruled by wicked philosophies. No historical phenomena, however, are meaningless when viewed in the light of Buddhist principles. Japan had suffered great misfortune, but the day was dawning when she would become Buddha's world. A nation embracing true Buddhism can turn poison into the elixir of life and misery and poverty into happiness and prosperity.[31]

Toda's self-appointed role was to start Japan on the road to peace and prosperity through Buddhism. One finds no such mission-statement in the writing of Makiguchi.

Another crucial contribution of Toda was his concept of obutsu myogo. Obutsu myogo is the belief that one cannot separate religion from society--that religion must serve as the foundation for other activities, and that a religion must send envoys into all spheres of activity, including politics. In a 1948 address on "The Way to the Restoration of the Nation," Toda noted

Philosophy must be the prerequisite of the restoration of the nation, but philosophy that is not backed up with practical action is no more than an intellectual game.... Today, when misleading religious sects and biased communist ideas are running rampant through society, we of Soka Gakkai, acting in conformity with the great philosophy of Nichiren Shoshu, must make the practical contributions to the rebuilding of our nation....In order to transform our defeated nation

> into a body of moral and peace-loving people, we must take it upon ourselves to remold politics, economics, and culture on the basis of the correct concepts of a correct religion. Only the Dai-Gohonzon and the philosophy of Nichiren Daishonin can be the foundation for the kind of nation Japan must become.[32]

Statements such as these laid the foundation for much of the Soka Gakkai's political activism that started in the early 1950s and which later led to the foundation of the Komeito in 1964.

Toda had fully developed the philosophical foundations for the new Soka Gakkai by the late 1940s, but he was much slower in expanding the organization physically. He was a businessman who before World War II had a fortune of more than six million yen, or $1.5 million at the official prewar exchange rate.[33] After the war Toda found that his prewar fortune was gone and that he was deeply in debt. He did everything possible to start up new businesses--he established correspondence schools, a school that taught English, several magazines, and a credit cooperative. These ventures enjoyed some early successes, but the incredibly high inflation after the war wiped out all his gains and forced him to shut down most of his operations.[34]

By devoting most of his attention to business, he could give the Soka Gakkai only partial attention. However, he supervised the founding of several chapters across Japan, formed such divisions as the Youth Division, held frequent discussion meetings, and lectured frequently on the Lotus Sutra.[35] Nevertheless, there were only about 3,000 members in the Gakkai by 1950. In terms of membership, the Gakkai ranked far behind such rivals as the Reiyukai and Rissho Koseikai.[36] It was not until the early 1950s that Toda abandoned his life as a businessman and put all of his efforts into the Soka Gakkai cause. It is interesting to note that the Gakkai's membership did not come from the greatly deprived people of the 1940s, but rather from the Japanese who did not benefit from the economic boom that occurred during the Korean War. However, this growth can be attributed to the structural foundations created by Toda in the late 1940s.

Thus, it was Toda that created both the philosophical and structural foundation for the Gakkai in the late 1940s. He was the combined philosopher, activist, and "fanatic" who molded the Gakkai's modern character.

## NOTES

[1]Muroo Tadashi, Soka Gakkai-Risho Koseikai (Tokyo, 1979), p. 22.

[2]Sugimori Koji, Kenkyu Soka Gakkai (Tokyo, 1976), p. 50.

[3]Quoted in H. Neill McFarland, The Rush Hour of the Gods (New York, 1967), p. 196.

[4]McFarland, p. 196.

[5]Ibid., p. 197

[6]Sugimori, pp. 47-48

[7]Ibid.

[8]Makiguchi Tsunesaburo, Kachiron (Tokyo, 1953), pp. 4-5.

[9]Makiguchi, pp. 4-19.

[10]Mitata Kiyoaki, Japan's New Buddhism (Tokyo, 1969), p. 77.

[11]Dayle M. Bethel, Makiguchi, The Value Creator (Tokyo, 1973), p. 56.

[12]Makiguchi, p. 5.

[13]Ibid., pp. 8-21.

[14]Ibid., pp. 178-81.

[15]Sugimori, p. 47.

[16]Makiguchi, The Philosophy of Value (Tokyo, 1964), p. 156.

[17]Ibid., p. 165.

[18]Ibid., p. 18.

[19]Murata, p. 18.

[20]Suematsu Yoshinori, "Makiguchi Sensei to Buppo to no deai," (Makiguchi's encounter with Buddhist Law) in Daibyaku Renge(June, 1976), pp. 20-23.

[21]Ibid.

[22]Toda Josei, Rombunshu (Tokyo, 1960), p. 204.

[23]Ibid.

[24]Kato Bunno et al., The Three-Fold Lotus Sutra (Tokyo, 1975), pp. 6-7.

[25]Toda, Rombunshu.

[26]Toda, Rombunshu, p. 13.

[27]Statement attributed to Toda in Ikeda Daisaku, The Human Revolution (Vol. II) (Tokyo, 1974), p. 5. The Human Revolution is Ikeda's semi-fictionalized history of the early years of the Soka Gakkai under Toda.

[28]Murata Kiyoaki, Japan's New Buddhism (Tokyo, 1969) p. 89.

[29]Toda Josei, "Seimei no Honshitsuron," (Thesis on the Essence of Life) which forms the first chapter of Shakubuku Kyoten (Shakubuku Manual), p. 3. Quoted in Murata, p. 89.

[30]Ikeda, Human Revolution (Vol. 1), p. 60.

[31]Ibid., pp. 69-70.

[32]Ikeda, Human Revolution (Vol. II), p. 89.

[33]Murata, p. 90.

[34]Ibid., pp. 89-93.

[35]See Higuma Takenori, Soka Gakkai Toda Josei (Tokyo, 1971), pp. 99-129.

[36]Sugimori, p. 51.

# CHAPTER 3

## THE SOKA GAKKAI'S SEARCH FOR THE REALIZATION
## OF THE WORLD OF RISSHO ANKOKU RON

The processes of innovation and the beliefs and related modes of behavior that led to acceptance or rejection of new ideas differ--sometimes extremely--from one culture to another, but such differences are as yet little understood. In every culture these processes and beliefs derive from premises that are very generalized and are expressed in behavior that is built-in from the earliest stages of an individual's learning experience. An understanding of the basic premises--and so of the processes, beliefs, and behavior--may be obtained by the following: studies of cultural character; analysis of the innovative individual and the cluster surrounding him or her; an investigation of the development of an institution's ideology.

In this chapter I have chosen the third course, and I shall discuss the Soka Gakkai movement's ideology and efforts to mold a new society in contemporary Japan in the light of the Japanese approach to the new and the old, the past and the present. The key to this central feature of Japanese society may be found in what the late Japanese philosopher Watsuji Tetsuro called the "stadial" character of Japanese society.[1]

## Stadiality

Stadiality refers to the successive layering effect, or stratification, of historical periods in Japanese history. No other major culture so readily assimilates new concepts while so loyally preserving the old and adapts to the new by turning to the past for inspiration. Older traditions, customs, and institutions are rarely, if ever, totally abandoned or rejected; instead, they continue to exist and affect contemporary behavior. Thus, the special character of contemporary Japanese culture derives from this accumulation and preservation of ideals and customs of past eras.

There are two essential aspects of the cultural stadiality: the negation of earlier traditions, and the permanent preservation of those traditions. In general, it is observable that any set of ideas and customs peculiarly characteristic of one era will be negated through the development of an opposite set in the next era. However, both systems--old and new--win a permanent place in Japanese culture and are assimilated by followers and students in succeeding periods. This little understood ability to negate the past and yet to preserve it by incorporation is what foreigners are referring to in calling Japan "a land of contradictions."

Stadiality is evident in every aspect of Japanese culture, including modes of dress, cuisine, and housing, in the historic transition of social classes, and in all the major social institutions. There is, for example, the survival of the imperial institution since very ancient times. Japan has been ruled by a single line of emperors without much of the frequent disruption of imperial lines so common in China and elsewhere. The Japanese emperors ceased having effective political power over a thousand years ago, as successive waves of military leaders, regents, and other officials took control of the government. Yet the imperial institution survived, often as a nearly forgotten relic of the past. Starting in the late 1860s, the leaders of the Meiji Restoration replaced the Tokugawa Shogunate with an imperial form of government. In theory, all authority was restored to the emperor, a subterfuge that permitted the effective government to initiate programs designed to modernize Japan.

Stadiality is also evident in popular culture. If one, for example, compares the aesthetic ideals expressed in Sei Shonagon's tenth century Pillow Book (Makura no Shoshi) and Yoshida Kenko's fourteenth century Essays in Idleness (Tsurezure-gusa), one sees a transition from a youth-oriented culture that cherished color, perfectibility, and regularity to one that favored the old, irregular, and imperfect. One today can find strains of both in Japanese culture.

Stadiality is also evident in religion. Many Japanese today still, at least nominally, follow Shinto, an ancient, primitive, polytheistic, and "this-worldly" religion in which man is closely associated with nature. In the seventh and eighth centuries, Shinto was displaced by several "other-worldly" Buddhist sects from China, and these in turn were displaced by succeeding waves of other Buddhist sects.[2] Yet today Shinto continues to play a major role in Japanese culture, and even the earliest Buddhist sects survive, although in very truncated form.

These historical examples of cultural stadiality demonstrate how the preservation of the past and the acceptance of older practices and ideals have resulted in a remarkable continuity in the midst of change in Japanese culture. They also demonstrate the source of the Soka Gakkai's eschatology. The Soka Gakkai has largely accepted Nichiren's assertion that the present world is heading toward disaster, but that with the proper religion, salvation and redemption are still possible.

Beneath all of its modern trappings, the Soka Gakkai promotes a very traditional program based on an ideology that partly dates back to the thirteenth century. Although it accepts and teaches the totality of its version of Nichiren's teachings, its religious program is based on its interpretation of two of Nichiren's treatises, the Kaimoku Sho and the Kanjin no Honzon Sho. Its social teachings are based firmly on the teachings found in Nichiren's <u>Rissho Ankoku Ron</u>, which serves as the blueprint for the Gakkai's social programs.

When Toda Josei was released from two years of solitary confinement in a Tokyo prison in 1945, he revealed to his family that he had undergone a profound religious experience. He saw a nation in ruins, a people desperate for hope. It is said that Toda was convinced that the cause of World War II was the same as that which had brought on all of Japan's disasters. Looking closely at what Nichiren wrote in <u>RAR</u>, and elsewhere, Toda felt he saw the reasons for Japan's "malady" as well as the cure. He built the Soka Gakkai to complete Nichiren's mission--the creation of a peaceful and prosperous nation or people. By looking back into the past for inspiration and guidance, Toda was responding to the stadial concepts so prevalent in Japanese society.[3]

## The Need for Social Reform

The eschatological view of history found in <u>RAR</u> led President Toda to realize that wherever he went, people seemed to be dominated by greed, anger, and sheer foolishness. Both rich and poor exhibited traits of haughtiness, jealousy, and pride. The individual was so obsessed with his own petty interests that he showed little concern for his neighbors. Each of the nation's leaders spoke of the need to reform and improve society, but perpetuated "scandalous politics" that brought out the worse in the citizenry."[4] Ikeda wrote:

> The root cause of the confusion of a nation is attributed to the disturbance of Buddhist Gods. Buddhist Gods here signify thought. When the right way of thinking is ignored, prejudiced views and ideologies begin to be accepted by the general public. Big-headed thinkers and critics display their

knowledge, sticking to their own opinions. When thought becomes chaotic, the people fall into disorder, and as they are disturbed, their country becomes agitated. Thus, the nation goes into ruin and the race suffers misery. This is the principle path to downfall.[5]

The Soka Gakkai also follows Nichiren's belief that national disaster can occur when a society refuses to accept the True Laws of Buddhism.[6] Nichiren talked in terms of natural disasters like earthquakes, but today the Soka Gakkai stresses that social problems rather than natural disasters are the indicators of the need for society to adopt the Gakkai's teachings.[7] Ikeda has gone so far as to say that Japan's defeat in the Pacific War was punishment for the Japanese government's suppression of Nichiren Shoshu and support for false religions during the war:

When the nation is disturbed, it will be attacked by the enemy and the people will suffer extreme hardships. In the Pacific War, the Japanese were in great consternation, just as they were in the Kamakura era when the Mongolian invaders ravaged the two islands, Iki and Tsushima, and also the coast of Kyushu...At that time Nichiren Daishonin was alive and defended this country, but in the time of the Pacific War, it went to wreck and ruin because the government oppressed Nichiren Shoshu and the Soka Gakkai.[8]

Ikeda describes Toda's thinking at the end of World War II:

Is there a religion in which one may safely put his trust? Yes. Seven hundred years ago, Nichiren Daishonin propounded the pure, true faith. But for all these long centuries people have turned deaf ears to his teachings. But at the end of the war, when the whole world had come to the sad state Nichiren Daishonin had prophesied, the age of awakening was close at hand...

The prophecy had at last come true. Japan, a nation 3,000 years old, lay prostrate. Nichiren Daishonin's vision had proved deadly accurate; and Toda was now convinced that the time had come for Nichiren

Shoshu to rise to full stature, for the founder had also foreseen the appearance of multitudes of followers of the true Buddhism who would come to the wasted land to propagate his teachings. At last all of Japan would know the unparalleled happiness achieved only when the true faith is spread to all people.[9]

False religion has led us to this cruel state... Japan had suffered great misfortune, but the day was dawning when she would become Buddha's world. A nation embracing true Buddhism can turn poison into the elixir of life and misery and poverty into happiness and prosperity.[10]

Thus, the Soka Gakkai grew after World War II with the goal of establishing Nichiren's world of RAR by moving the people away from false beliefs to the only "true Buddhism." It describes its mission from the vantage point of stadiality. Nichiren's view of destruction and chaos and its causes is carried by his Soka Gakkai followers today. The Soka Gakkai adapts itself to the postwar environment of Japan by turning back to the past for answers. The Soka Gakkai's innovative programs today draw strongly on Nichiren Shoshu's interpretations of Nichiren's prognosis of Japan's ills.

The major thrust of the Soka Gakkai's philosophy is that we still do live during the age of mappo. Rissho Ankoku Ron represents society as it could be but is not now. We can move to the world of RAR here and now--not in some distant paradise after death--if we would change our karmas by worshipping the true religion of Nichiren Shoshu. Society will remain full of evil and strife as long as we continue to ignore the Soka Gakkai's dire warnings. Japan suffered from the hell of World War II because of its failure to follow Nichiren's teachings. The world today might experience a total eclipse from nuclear war if we fail to listen to Ikeda's teachings on religion and peace. Even if we live in a comparative peace, Soka Gakkai President Akiya states that we all suffer from a significant degree of spiritual poverty. Modern problems include crime, the drug culture, and general apathy among the people.[11] Here again we see stadiality at work.

## The Soka Gakkai's Peace Movement

The Soka Gakkai has initiated many active social programs to realize RAR. The venture into politics which led to the creation of the Komeito, for example, was done to purify Japan's corrupt political environment, to remove much of the intolerance that had shaped the government's attitudes towards its religion. The Soka Gakkai today has an ardent "Peace Movement" (heiwa undo) that is meant to help man find the tranquility possible in Nichiren's utopian vision of RAR. The peace movement is a new and innovative program, but its inspiration and direction come from RAR--another clear example of how stadiality is used to promote new programs by turning back to the past.

Today the SG regards its peace movement as perhaps its most important activity in its search for the world of RAR. The character of the Gakkai's peace movement, which is built on its eschatological view of world politics, is based on the premise that enduring peace will be achieved only when there is a fundamental change in man's character. Man is plagued by evil karma and is thus trapped in a world of misery and suffering. His fate and state in life can be improved only if there is an improvement in his karma. According to the Soka Gakkai, the only way to improve karma is to worship the Daigohonzon, a mandala which Nichiren is said to have inscribed shortly before his death in 1282. Nichiren Shoshu insists that the Daigohonzon is imbued with the saving powers of the true Buddha of the Latter Day. All who pray before the mandala will be saved if they have faith. Likewise, society has a collective karma composed of all the individual karmas that constitute its makeup. Thus, the quality of society will improve as individual karmas improve. A person with a bad karma is prone to violence and hate; good karma people stress peace and love. The only way to arrive at world peace is to gradually improve the karmas of all men, and world peace "can never be attained without the Buddhism of Nichiren Daishonin."[12] Since it believes that it has the key to the improvement of karma and thence the salvation of mankind, the SG claims that it has the world's only genuine and effective peace movement.

Ikeda, like Toda, uses stadiality by referring back to RAR to bolster his own program for world peace:

> The core of the message of the Rissho Ankoku Ron is this: on a national, international, or worldwide scale, the only way to bring about lasting peace is to establish the reign of the true Buddhist Law. This work, Nichiren's first active approach to social problems, and the establishment of the Daigohonzon, the embodiment of peaceful wishes for all people, were profound reasons for Nichiren's appearance on this earth. In these things he showed that the ideal and true spirit of practical Buddhist action in society is the realization of lasting peace for all mankind....The keynote of the Soka Gakkai lies in the realization of the spiritual and material happiness of the individual through...faith, practice and study, as well as in the advancement of peace and culture for society as a whole. This is the true spirit embodied in Nichiren Daishonin's essay entitled Rissho Ankoku Ron.

> The most horrible of war's aspects is probably not the cruelty and evil of its effects, but the fact that it brings to the forefront the vilest, most atrocious elements of human life. War strips loftiness and respect from humanity and, through its wicked actions, covers man with filth. It is only natural that Buddhism, the aim of which is to guide people to the highest, purest realms, is bound to oppose war directly. By a like token, the Buddhist believer who is

eager to practice his faith in the truest way regards it as his mission to pour his entire soul into the task of building peace.[13]

The Soka Gakkai feels that it has the answer to peace. It has defined peace as a harmonious way of life that is devoid of war. In other words, it is the creation of a better world, which to some extent resembles the Kingdom of God expressed in eschatological accounts in the Bible. In Ikeda's words, "Peace ought not to be thought of as a brief period of respite between wars."[14] Just as Nichiren petitioned the government with a diagnosis and cure for the problems of war facing Japan seven centuries ago, the Soka Gakkai peace movement intends to educate mankind about the horror of war and then to show him how Buddhism can bring him eternal peace.

The peace movement of the Soka Gakkai consists of a variety of activities focusing on peace education, support of the United Nations, aid to refugees, and attempts at personal diplomacy. Although the movement has brought about some public skepticism and is not without its detractors, this movement has changed the attitudes of at least some Gakkai members in that they seem to have a "peace consciousness" that may not have been as strong before they knew about the peace movement.

In its politics and in its peace education program, the Gakkai has adopted the polemical style of Nichiren. Just as Nichiren acted as a social and political gadfly in opposing the policies of the government of his day when he wrote RAR, the Soka Gakkai's political party has consistently been a leader among the ranks of the opposition, and its peace education program has adopted Nichiren's urgent tone. Just as Nichiren appointed himself as a spokesman for the people, the Soka Gakkai has appointed itself as the guardian of the people and as such is guiding them to a world of peace.[15]

The Soka Gakkai's peace education program has led to the publication of a multi-volume series of books recounting the first-hand experiences of Japanese during World War II. In the 1970s, members of the Soka Gakkai's Youth and Women's Divisions canvassed many older Japanese and collected a broad range of wartime experiences. These memories were published in a 56 volume series, Sensoo o Shiranai Sedai e (To the Generations Who Do Not Know War). The point of this series is to remind people of the horror of World War II and to instruct the younger generation of Japanese, who know little of World War II. One fifth grade student in Japan was amazed when I told her that Americans and Japanese had been deadly enemies only forty years ago. Japanese history textbooks used by Japanese high school students today only devote six pages to World War II and a minuscule two or three paragraphs to the atomic bombing of Hiroshima and Nagasaki.[16]

The Soka Gakkai's antiwar books consist of a series of ten page essays. The goal is to reinforce the eschatological view of war as symbolic of the hell that exists in so many people's minds. The tone of the essays is typified by the memories of a Japanese army officer who spent much of the war in China. while preparing to march one morning, he recalls:

> It was announced suddenly that three men were missing from another organization. At once our commander called the march off and ordered us to search for the missing soldiers. Leaving our men behind, we set off in all directions. At about three in the afternoon, we found the three corpses in the bottom of a valley.

They had been stripped stark naked and tied with wires. Their ears and noses had been cut off; their eyes stared emptily until some of us gently stroked them shut. Wrath and hatred for people who could do such a thing made us tremble as we wordlessly prayed for the repose of the dead men.

But they had not been killed without cause. In China, the Japanese pursued a policy of destruction and death--the policy was applied with special stringency in dealing with partisans. We soldiers were instructed to kill, burn and steal wherever we went. On the night before their deaths, these soldiers had sneaked away from camp to rob Chinese in the neighborhood of their hard-earned, scarce food. They had been caught, mutilated, and killed for their attempted robbery.

Our enraged commander ordered us to burn the nearby village in retaliation. Hundreds of Chinese lives were to be taken to pay for the three murders. To me, as one of the soldiers, what happened next seems to be spontaneous fury. Our men surrounded the village of about 200 houses on three sides, leaving one side open as an escape way. Probably this kind of thing happened in other operations and organizations. I had seen how cruel the Chinese could be to Japanese soldiers. Though I could not understand the sense of killing the ignorant inhabitants of 200 houses, I had no choice but to follow orders and help pile up straw tinder for the coming conflagration.

Tongues of fire leaped from the ignited straw and lapped the roofs. Soon the entire settlement was ablaze with roaring flames from three sides. Screams of frightened Chinese filled the air. We set up light and heavy guns on the fourth--the escape side--and waited. Before long they came: rushing and shrieking to escape, young men and women in the front, old people and children in the rear. Some were aflame. Some old people stumbled. Nervous as if bewitched, I had no time to doubt the justice of our acts or even to think. We opened merciless fire on the frantic Chinese who, under the deadly rain of bullets, were soon a pile of corpses.

Everything was over in a flash. From the village, an unearthly heap of rubble, flames still writhed upward. Its inhabitants lay scattered about, burned black or riddled with bullet holes. Somehow I could not believe that it had happened. Innocent people! Sobered by the bewitchment that had gripped me a few minutes earlier, once again I was beset by doubts about our actions. But I had to stifle them because we were already ordered to move out for the next encounter.

The destruction of the village, ostensible in vengeance for the murder of three Japanese soldiers, fitted well into the general Japanese policy of kill, burn and steal. Was this gong on all over China? Was Chinese blood being drained at this rate, everywhere? I could not put such cruelty down as mere good, brave military strategy.[17]

The main value of such antiwar publications is the emotional reaction that they can provoke. Their scholarly value is limited because the essays are placed in the books in a rather haphazard manner with no attempt at analysis. There is a great need for some discussion of the causes of war. It is valid to say that war is horrible and to remind people of these horrors, but one needs to go much deeper. And yet since Japanese textbooks almost completely ignore the last war, these books might give younger Japanese some sense of what is was like to live through World War II in Japan.

The Soka Gakkai also has put together a series of exhibitions depicting the ugliness and terror of war. One exhibition, "The Nuclear Threat to the World," was held at the United Nations several years ago and has subsequently been shown throughout Europe, Japan, and China.[18] There is a permanent exhibit of nuclear horrors run by the Soka Gakkai outside of its headquarters in Yokohama. This exhibit not only contains the expected pictures of Nagasaki and Hiroshima and eye-witness accounts of the death and destruction there, but it also depicts the current power of nuclear weapons.

The Soka Gakkai is putting on exhibits about war in some of its regional headquarters. The Women's Peace Committee in Fukuoka has been holding exhibits for four years with new exhibits every six months. One particular exhibit is said to have attracted up to 140,000 visitors during July of 1984. This exhibit featured the experiences and feelings of Japanese women at home while their husbands, father, sons, and brothers were fighting in China and elsewhere. On display were pictures, artifacts, and stories documenting the hardships faced at home, as well as at the front. In addition, a film taken in Nagasaki during the atomic bombing was shown, and a scale model of Fukuoka showing how lethal a similar bomb would have been had it hit there was displayed. According to a member of the Women's Peace Committee:

> We had considerable difficulty in organizing this exhibit, and it took some ingenuity to succeed. One problem is a lack of funds. We had to do a lot with very little. We went to the local newspaper and got many pictures from their morgue. We borrowed and copied many pictures at low cost. We talked to many older women in our neighborhoods and got descriptions of the war as well as some artifacts that they had saved. At first the survivors of the War were quite reluctant to talk, but when they saw the earnestness of our purpose, they seemed eager to help us. We approached authorities in a museum in Nagasaki and easily persuaded them to let us borrow a copy of their film on the Nagasaki bombing.[18]

Apparently, no school groups came to see the exhibit, but some teachers, as well as parents with their children, came. Despite the relatively small number of people who saw it, this exhibit is significant. The organizers of the exhibit said that they had received no appreciable training in history and had known very

52

little about World War II, since the oldest member had been a child during the war.  By building their own exhibit, these women were forced to learn a great deal about the war.  More importantly, it made them feel as if they were doing something constructive to end the horror of war.  One member stated:

> There is so little that we as individuals can do.  But working together we can produce exhibits that tell our neighbors about the horrors of war.  This sense of accomplishment encourages us by heightening our desire for peace and our support for the peace efforts of Ikeda Daisaku. [19]

On the other hand, it is hard to measure the effect that the education program has had on the average member.  When I talked about the peace movement with hundreds of Soka Gakkai members, I was told that all of them genuinely favor peace, but it is difficult for me to measure the depth of this support.  Soka Gakkai leaders sternly admonish members who are not studying peace material published by the Soka Gakkai.  At one study meeting of Soka Gakkai Youth Division members at the main temple of Taiseki-ji, a Soka Gakkai official admonished students who had not read from an assigned book written by Ikeda Daisaku: "We are the harbingers of peace, but how can we succeed if you are so complacent?  Today we live in a rich and conservative country that is deliberately ignoring the threat to peace and life imposed by nuclear weapons.  Only hard work on your part can start the process of public awareness of the horrors of war."[20]

The peace movement, on the other hand, seems to have somewhat radicalized some of the Soka Gakkai's leaders.  For example, there seems to be growing opposition in the Soka Gakkai to the Komeito's support for the United States-Japan Treaty.  Party Secretary Yano Junya supported the treaty because of the necessity of maintaining friendly relations with the United

States in order to ensure Japan's peace and security.[21] Younger party activists campaigning against the deployment of Tomahawk missiles and nuclear weapons have complained that the party is attaching too much importance to the security pact's virtue as a deterrent since the danger is growing that Japan may become embroiled in a war because of the treaty. These protests forced the Komeito to begin a formal review of its policy towards the Security Treaty. If the activists do get the party to reverse its stand, then the peace movement will have had some effect on Japanese politics. Other Soka Gakkai leaders seem to have been radicalized by the peace movement in the sense that they are taking a more hostile stance towards their government's defense politics and towards the nuclear and foreign policies of the Reagan administration. Many of these same people supported the re-election of Gerald Ford nine years ago because he was "harmless."[22]

### Other Efforts at Peaceful Reform

The Soka Gakkai is also apparently making an effort to foster member and public awareness of the United Nations. The Soka Gakkai was registered as a non government organization (NGO) associated with the UN Department of Public Information, and as an NGO it is supposed to assume the task of redisseminatin information to a wider public. The Soka Gakkai claims that it is furthering the cause of the UN by its attendance at annual NGO conferences, by its contributions to the UN Oral History Project, by its presentation of the exhibit, "We and the United Nations" at sites all over Japan, and by its public forums where support for the UN is urged.[23]

The Soka Gakkai has also donated about half a million dollars for refugees since 1981. The money, which has been given to the United Nations Commissioner for Refugees (UNHCR), was raised primarily by "on the street" fund-raising by younger members.[24] One can readily find printed Soka Gakkai material that attempts to focus public attention on the plight, needs, and problems of refugees.[25] Various divisions of the Soka Gakkai have published pamphlets outlining the basic requirements for a good diet, showing where food for such a diet is grown, and describing deficiencies in the diets of people in much of the Third World. The point made is that hunger today is a real problem, that hungry humans are living in a very real hell, and that it is the duty and obligation of those in wealthier nations to help the less fortunate.[26]

Again, one sees an effort by the Soka Gakkai to involve its ordinary members in the peace education process. This not only further binds them to the Soka Gakkai, but encourages them to feel that they are playing a role in the peace process. A half-million dollars is not a great sum of money, but it can do some good, and it does provide members who donate money and time a sense of accomplishment.

## Conclusion

Nichiren's themes of Rissho Ankoku Ron are still very much alive in the Soka Gakkai. Nichiren saw a nation living through difficult times and made a genuine effort to improve conditions for the Japanese. He believed that the only cure could come through the religious practices and beliefs of the people. Attention to "false religions" and neglect of the "highest" and "truest" form of Buddhism led to endless misery. Thus, Nichiren felt that it was necessary to alert the Japanese government to the severity of the problem and to urge it to stop supporting the "false religions." Nichiren suffered continual persecution as a result, but the more he was persecuted, the more he believed in the correctness of his cause. Nichiren proclaimed that in turning to the correct religion, man could live in a more peaceful and harmonious world.

Despite the apparent success and prosperity of the Japanese, the Soka Gakkai sees much misery in the world and genuine threats to world peace. This is hardly a novel or startling conclusion, but its diagnosis is more unique. The Gakkai's view of the cause of the problem is the same as that of Nichiren: Japan's defeat and misery in World War II came as a result of the Japanese government's support for the "true" Buddhism of Nichiren, and its persecution of followers of the Nichiren Sho sect and Gakkai leaders and members during the war. The gods have not yet returned to Japan in the postwar era, and as a result, Japan is vulnerable to threats from within and without.

The Soka Gakkai seeks to educate the world about the efficacy of its form of Buddhism. Nichiren appealed directly to the Japanese government because of its power to influence Buddhist sects. The Soka Gakkai states that since the government is now chosen by the people in elections, it needs to appeal to and educate the public as a whole if it is to have any public influence. It sees the treatment it receives from the Japanese press as symbolic of the persecution leveled against Nichiren and is determined, like its mentor, to continue fighting for the cause it sees as just. It is convinced that the era of mappo can be brought to an end and that the Soka Gakkai is the force that can lead man through the darkness and evil of this age into an enlightened period of peace, harmony, and great human creativity. In this sense, the Soka Gakkai's attempts to inherit Nichiren's cloak of RAR is very real.

Much of the current success of the Soka Gakkai can be attributed to the manner in which stadiality is used. Its leaders have built a modern mass movement and a strong political party not through the promotion of modern ideas, but by looking back at doctrines that were clearly espoused by a figure in the past. The Soka Gakkai is not simply paying lip-service to Nichiren and his idea; these ideas from the very basis of the Gakkai's social program, which is working for such modern achievements as the attainment of political power in the Diet.  Much of the Soka Gakkai's own popularity also stems from a sense of security--the Soka Gakkai promises modern rewards, but its premise is traditional.

# NOTES

[1]The origin of this metamorphic use of a term is in modern geology. As defined in Webster's Third New International Dictionary (1965), a stadial is a "substage of a glacial state, especially one marked by a readvancement of ice." There is, in fact, no other more specific term in English for the phenomenon to which Watsuji Tetsuro refers and which is under discussion in this paper.

I was introduced to Watsjui Tetsuro's work through a series of lectures by Professor David Dilworth at Columbia University in March, 1973, and through Professor Dilworth's draft translation of Watsuji's The Stadial Character of Japanese Society.

[2]The Esoteric Buddhism of the Heian era (794-1185) emphasized the idea that art is the medium through which enlightenment can be communicated. There was a cult of beauty and "this-worldliness." Each individual was believed to have the Buddha-nature in him and could achieve enlightenment on earth. It was an optimistic age in which aesthetic appreciation had quasi-religious overtones in the Japanese court.

[3]The Pure Land sects of the Kamakura period (1185-1333) were in many respects a negation of the Tendai and Shingon Buddhism of the Heian era. Pure Land Buddhism taught that man lives in a world of ugliness and sin and, having no power to save himself, must put total reliance in the Buddha Amida for salvation. Man cannot find peace and tranquility on earth but only in the Western Paradise after death.

[4]Sugimori Koji, Kenkyu Soka Gakkai (Tokyo, 1976), pp. 49-63.

[5]Toda Josei, Kantogenshu (Tokyo, 1960), pp. 200-1 and 209-10.

[6]Ikeda Daisaku, Lectures on Buddism (Vol. 2) (Tokyo, 1962), p. 279.

[7]Ibid., pp. 275-76.

[8]Interview with Harada Minoru (Director of Youth and Student Divisions of the SG), 8 August 1976 in Hokkaido.

[9]Ikeda, Lectures, pp. 278-80.

[10]Ikeda Daisaku, The Human Revolution (Vol. 1) (Tokyo, 1972), p. 48.

[11]Ibid., p. 48 and pp. 69-70.

[12]Interview with President Akiya in Tokyo, March 20, 1987.

[13]Interview with a member of the SG's Young Women's Division, June 17, 1984, in Yokohama. All ten women being interviewed strongly agreed with this assertion.

[14]Ikeda, A Lasting Peace (Tokyo, 1981), pp. 21-22 and p. 237.

[15]Interview between author and Ikeda at Soka University, July 15, 1984.

[16]See Kasahara Ichiro et al., Nihonshi (Tokyo, 1975 and 1984).

[17]Youth Division of Soka Gakkai, Peace is Our Duty (Tokyo, 1982), pp. 39-41.

[18]The exhibit was sponsored by the United Nations Department of Public Information with the support of the Soka Gakkai and the cities of Hiroshima and Nagasaki, but most of the material shown and much of the funding and preparation were provided by the Soka Gakkai.

[19]Interview with members of the Soka Gakkai Fukuoka Women's Peace Committee, June 28, 1984 in Fukuoka.

[20]Ibid.

[21]From the talk to a group of Soka Gakkai Young Men's Division Members by a group leader. July 24, 1985 at Taiseki-ji, head temple of Nichiren Shoshu.

[22]Interview with Yano Junya, Secretary General of the Komeito and member of the Lower House of the Diet, July 30, 1984.

[23]"Clean Government Party to Revise its Security Policy," in the Asahi Evening News, July 30, 1984, p. 1.

[24]Soka Gakkai International, "In Pursuit of Lasting Peace," (Tokyo, 1983). Pamphlet. According to the Japan Times of July 6, 1984, the Soka Gakkai made another donation of $433,000 that day to the UN.

[25]Ibid.

[26]Youth Division (of SG) of Aichi Prefecture, "Tabemono: Genzai Shorai."

# CHAPTER 4

## SUFFERING AS A MOTIVATION FOR MEMBERSHIP

The eschatological ideas and beliefs of mappo center on the pain of human suffering. In a time when it is said that the people are losing touch with the Salvationist teachings of the Buddha, individuals, as well as society as a whole, are experiencing hardship. Suffering is both physical and mental as the tragedies of war, disease, natural disasters, and hunger afflict mankind. Mental torment includes financial distress, bad marriages, the breakup of the family, unemployment, and general apathy.[1] Even with relative economic prosperity, a nation that has a sizeable number of these afflictions truly can be said to be living in mappo.

The Soka Gakkai insists that many of these problems are caused by bad karma and that these outward indicators of mappo will largely disappear if and when society adopts of "true Buddhism." All suffering, of course, will not come to an end. People will always experience the inevitable cycle of birth and death, but their lives will be much richer and happier with Nichiren's Buddhism.[2] Without the help of Nichiren Buddhism, Gakkai leaders stress that karmas will remain tainted, which will foster hatred and greed among men.

Most of the several hundred Soka Gakkai members I interviewed over the past decade say that they were suffering from some physical or psychological problem or problems when they joined the Soka Gakkai. The usual sequence of events is for the Soka Gakkai member to approach a person in anguish to tell him that the "true Buddhism" of Nichiren can bring an end to pain.

After considerable persuasion, the sufferer joins the movement. In time, the power of the "true Buddhism" takes effect and the pain ends.

The Soka Gakkai regards itself as Nichiren's successor, charged with the task of realizing his mission by spreading his word throughout the world. The dream is the realization of Nichiren's vision of Rissho Ankoku Ron, where eternal peace will reign and greed and hatred will disappear from the hearts of man. The means to this goal is the Human Revolution (ningen kakumei), which is the purification of one's karma through faith and practice. This consists of absolute acceptance of the truth of Nichiren's teachings as interpreted by Nichiren Shoshu and the Soka Gakkai, constant prayer (gongyo), and proselytization of the faith (shakubuku). When one advances forward through the Ten Worlds towards Buddhahood through the cleansing of one's karma, one becomes a much happier, healthier, more confident individual. When many people in society improve their karmas and social karma approaches Buddhahood, the world will become a far better and more peaceful place. This will be the realization of Rissho Ankoku Ron.

The Soka Gakkai feels that RAR will be found through a step-by-step process through the conversion of believers individual by individual. This is done by shakubuku, which is today the gentle persuasion used by a member to convince a nonbeliever of the great benefits of the religion and to get him to join. Shakubuku has two forms: the one-to-one contact between a member and nonmember and the group contact that a guest would have at a zadankai.

When studying the Gakkai, one gets the strong impression that the average member who was not brought up from birth in a Soka Gakkai family was almost always a dissatisfied person before joining. James White grouped motives for entry into the Soka Gakkai into three main categories: illness, poverty, and conflict.[3] Surveys conducted by James White in the 1960s found that roughly a fifth of the members interviewed gave illness as the major motive for entry. About 14 percent gave poverty as a reason while another third gave conflict as the principal reason. These results suggested to White that social causes have figured largely in the growth of the Gakkai.[4]

There are occasional individuals who enter the Soka Gakkai merely out of curiosity, because a friend or relative had joined, because of interest, or because they are impressed with the size, power, and magnetism of the movement. However, virtually everybody who joined the movement on his own and who had no friends or relatives who were already a part of the Gakkai did so because of some degree of suffering.

My own interviews with about fifty Soka Gakkai members in 1984 and 1985 confirm White's findings to an extent, but a fourth category that White does not mention is lack of confidence. Many of those whom I interviewed said that they were emotionally and physically sound but were going nowhere in life because of a lack of confidence in themselves. They did not have the courage or determination to improve their lives, to try something new or different. Soka Gakkai members approached them and urged them to exert themselves in ways they had never done before. Responses to my survey as to why a person joined the Gakkai can be summarized as follows:[5]

Social reasons = 25%
Lack of confidence = 40%
Economic motivation = 10%
Illness = 25%

Thus, those who joined the Soka Gakkai because of financial or physical problems constituted about one-third of the members while two-thirds joined because they felt that their own personalities or social relationships would be transformed or improved through some form of human revolution. Membership was accepted when they realized that activities and friendships within the Soka Gakkai somehow led to a relaxation or elimination of their problem.

Members and converts are often told that suffering is necessary because it teaches you how to overcome adversity. You are also told that the cause of the problem lies within yourself. You cannot blame others for your misfortune; rather, you must "clear up your own act" if you are to overcome your problems: If you are sick, it is because of bad karma within yourself. If you are a failure in business, it is because bad karma clouded your good judgment and led you to make disastrous mistakes. Bad karma can only be overcome through chanting and shakubuku. Chanting before a gohonzon cleanses the karma, a process that is reinforced by spreading the good word to others. You are also taught that the cleansing of karma (human revolution) is a slow gradual process. Failure to chant or proselytize even after years of practice can lead to a recurrence of problems or the start of new ones. Good karma will give you the ability to overcome many diseases, the courage to tackle any financial problem however grave, the strength and bravery to enter new jobs or careers, and the wisdom to succeed. You will be able to make new friends, solve many problems in marriage and be happy, but you cannot cease praying at any time. Faith and proselytization are ongoing activities that Soka Gakkai members cannot abandon.

Obviously not all members find success or happiness in the Soka Gakkai and some abandon their practice. According to one speaker at a Gakkai block-meeting in Tokyo in 1984, failure of a member to achieve happiness was due to the following:

> Their practice and faith was not complete. They lacked the strength and conviction so necessary for success. Not all of us in this room have total success or happiness even now. Some of us pray and yet still have problems.
>
> When I talk to these people about their attitudes, I note an escapist tendency. They blame others for their problems when the fault is, in fact, in them. They chant outwardly but let their minds drift. We must be brave; a coward cannot chant. You should use suffering as a stepping-stone to deepen your faith.
>
> We all want protection; we all face hard futures from which there is no escape. Others cannot solve your own problems. We must solve them ourselves. We must be disciplined; escape solves no problems. Be as strong outside as you are inside. As long as you run away, you will be chased after. You can change your own attitude through chanting and shakubuku."

Another official told members at the same block-meeting in 1984 that they were all envoys (Bodhisattvas) of the Buddha with a sacred duty to spread the good word. When Nichiren was alive, it took a considerable amount of suffering, including persecution and ridicule from others, to make him realize that he was the true Buddha. The mission of Nichiren was to teach us the way to happiness and to bring peace to the world. Bodhisattvas are self-motivated and courageous people whose mission is to spread happiness to others and to blaze the path to world peace. Prayer gives us much energy. "Chanting the daimoku gives us peace and happiness NOW."

Cures from illness provide the most dramatic cases of the decision to become a Soka Gakkai member. The following four cases are typical.

[1]    A woman in her mid-thirties at another block-meeting in 1984 notes:

> I became a member quite a while ago, but my husband was not a member. I have gained much confidence and happiness as a result.
>
> Five years ago my husband developed a pancreatic disease which, next to pancreatic cancer, is the most severe and painful. He was taken to a hospital in an ambulance. I chanted long and hard for his recovery. He was impressed with my earnestness and to my utter surprise and delight asked for the gohonzon and began to chant on his own. Tears flowed down my cheeks.
>
> To my delight my husband began to get better and the doctors were astounded. The initial operation had not been too successful, but the second one was. I was eight months pregnant and was terrified that my husband would not live to see the birth of our child and that my worry would itself cause a difficult birth. But the baby was born successfully, and my husband was getting better day by day. My mother encouraged prayer and chanting to change my karma. I was able to later convert my sister-in-law and her husband. Through suffering one is taught the benefits of faith, prayer, chanting and shakubuku.

[2]    A middle-aged man stated that he had been a member of the Soka Gakkai prior to his coming to Tokyo in the late 1960s, but after his arrival he virtually abandoned the practice. After he was married he began to feel rather ill. When he went to the doctor and was given a series of tests, he was told that he had a rare and incurable form of cancer. Remembering what he had been taught by the Soka Gakkai, he went back to earnest practice of the two basic elements of the religion--chanting and proselytization, whereupon he began to win the battle against his disease. "I came to realize that practice and devotion to the gohonzon can overcome all obstacles. Suffering is necessary

because it teaches one to overcome adversity. All suffering can be overcome. Chanting is a crucial part to curing disease."

[3] A middle-aged contractor who had just become a member stated that he had been hurt on a number of occasions in work-related accidents, but after joining he had fallen off a high ladder and was not even bruised.

[4] An older woman stated that she had been a member for a very long time, but that around the age of forty she had swayed from the faith. The result was disastrous for her family.

> There was a bad traffic accident in the family, my husband got cancer, and my father began suffering from a great illness. Luckily I quickly recognized the error of my ways and had the conviction to overcome all of this through chanting, faith and practice. We were soon able to convert a friend and her husband and my husband and father began to practice this religion. Thus my husband was able to overcome his illness and my father could die in peace.

Financial distress and lack of confidence, coupled with encouragement from Soka Gakkai members that religious practice could lead to an end to problems, led many people to membership. The following three cases are examples:

[1} A man in his mid-fifties stated that when he first came to Tokyo in 1961, he was arrogant and had a brash character. At one point he was approached by a Soka Gakkai member who made a wager with him--they would work to see who could convert the other to his religion first. After that the Soka Gakkai member left him alone. The man quickly set up a small business that led to a joint-venture with another businessman; quick failure and devastating bankruptcy ensued:

> I had lost everything. I had huge debts and was badly malnourished. I was standing alone on a bridge one evening in deep depression when the

Soka Gakkai member approached me, put his arm around me, and said that there was always hope, that debts could be paid and good health found. He said that he was praying for me, but that I had to pray too. I was reminded of Toda's suffering and his recovery of health. I then cnverted to this religion and practiced hard by chanting and being engaged in shakubuku. I soon found a good job and kept my faith despite taunts from my boss and co-workers. Later I found even a better job and was able to repay all debts. Now I have a wonderful religion, a good job, and a suitable amount of money in the bank. I am very happy. More than anything this religion gave me the courage and optimism I needed to carry on.

[2] A slightly younger man said that he had been involved in the textile industry in Nagoya in the 1960s and 1970s but had lost his job due to the collapse of the Japanese textile industry. In despair he turned to his religion for help and began fervent chanting. He thereby regained the confidence he needed to succeed:

I was told by the district leader that if you cannot stand up for yourself, nobody will do it for you. That gave me the courage to continue. Soon thereafter a friend who owned a small clothing store opened a second branch and asked me to run it. Under my management the branch store prospered. My friend also let me rent a small house that he owned at a very reasonable rate. My wife and I had no children up to then, but soon we had a little girl. It was later suggested that I seek a pharmaceutical license, so after work I began taking courses at a pharmaceutical college. Thus I had an active life of hard work in the store, study after hours, and active practice in religion. In time I graduated from school, passed the exam, and got the license. Later I opened a small Tokyo supermarket called Superstore Hope. Business has been very good and the store is rapidly expanding.

The man pointed out the window to the Superstore Hope located down the street. One could see bright lights, a great deal of produce inside, and many people coming and going, even at 9:00 at night.

[3] A local leader of the Women's Division said that she met an older woman who seemed greatly depressed. This older woman said that the cause of her misery was that she and her husband were deeply in debt. "I told her that if she were devout in her practice and faith, debt collectors would no longer bother her. When she did what I said, they stopped coming absolutely."

While emotional distress accompanied the financial worries and physical suffering of members, a few had worries that were not based on problems of finance or disease. Part of the appeal of the Soka Gakkai has been its ability to give solace and self-confidence to individuals cut adrift in a collective group society. After World War II, the demographic picture of Japan changed substantially. People left their rural villages and moved to cities, but many new arrivals to the cities were cut off from their village temples and shrines and from family ties. If they were self-employed or worked for a small commercial establishment, they did not automatically belong to a recognizable group. The Soka Gakkai and other new religions provided them with a religious base, as well as a group they could join.

People who join the Soka Gakkai for emotional reasons often say that they were lonely and depressed. Quite often they mention being insecure, shy, and without much ambition in life. Somehow they encounter Soka Gakkai members who seem happy, goal-oriented people. The happiness of the member, as well as his suggestion that entry into this new religion will make the nonmember really happy, encourages membership. One famous television actress notes:

Since my parents were members, I was also a Soka Gakkai member since childhood, but I was not what one could call a devout member. I went to a Christian high school, although I was not an actual Christian. At that school I had a friend who was very troubled. I sent her to my mother who was a devout member. She helped her overcome her problems. Through the strength of my friend's problems I saw the meaning of faith and practice and became an active believer. This in turn allowed me to overcome my lack of self-confidence and allowed me to grow to take on the challenges of a hard and strong acting career.

A young woman who was a sophomore at Japan's Waseda University joined because a Soka Gakkai member helped her during the critical period of taking the very difficult entrance exam to that school:

When I took the exam for the first time three years ago I failed badly. I became a wandering student (ronin) with no clear goals in life. I was deeply discouraged and depressed. A practicing member urged me to chant and to study hard for the next exam. I was deeply impressed with the high morale and great warmth of the members I came to know during that year. When I took the exam for the second time my member-friend said that she had been actively praying for my success. I was deeply moved. I was stunned when the results came in telling me that I had passed. I went to my friend and asked how I could pay her back. I was told that the best payment would be for me to practice as well.

A housewife said that due to economic necessity she was forced to go back to work a few years ago, but she had no place to put her very young children. Local authorities said there were no available slots in local day-care centers or kindergartens. She chanted, hoping that a place could be found. Within forty-eight hours she received word that two separate slots had been found. Now she is able to work full-time in the family business.

One can get a more complete view of the life of a Soka Gakkai family by reading the "Experiences" column printed in the Soka Gakkai's newspaper, the Seikyo Shimbun. These inspirational stories are printed to demonstrate the strength of the religion for its believers. They serve the same purpose as the personal testimonials and professions of faith found at every zadankai, at which people unburden themselves before a sympathetic audience. Each of these "Experiences" is upbeat in tone; a former nonbeliever suffers some calamity, but the sympathetic Soka Gakkai member is always there to lend a sympathetic hand--to shakubuku him and to lead him to happiness and greater wealth through the true teaching of Nichiren. The following story appeared in the Seikyo Shimbumn recently:

### BUDDHIST SPIRIT OF CHALLENGE ENABLES
### FAMILY TO CHANGE FATE

Landward, the fishing port of Shitsukari on the Pacific side of the Shimokia Peninsula in the northern part of Aomori Prefecture is encircled by steep cliffs. It is a small port, hit directly by the rolling waves of the Pacific Ocean, so much so that in the early days fishermen could not put out to sea in slightly heavy weather.

Mr. Kiyoharu Ogasawara, 33, a group chief of a Soka Gakkai district organization in the area, recalls: `During the times of my father, it was really a poor fishing village, with people finding it very hard to make a living. To make matters worse for us, my younger brother Hisao was afflicted with nephrosis, a serious kidney ailment, and the doctor said he had almost no hope of recovering.'

Despite the doctor's pronouncement, the entire family wanted to do whatever they could for him. In order to cover the hospital expense, they cut down and sold the cypress and cedar from the family forest. In the spring of 1962, the father, Sueji, left home to work in Hakodate in Hokkaido, across the strait, to make extra money.

Working away from home for the first time in his life, the father endured the hard labor of road construction, to which he was not accustomed. Autumn came and the work having been completed, the father prepared to return home after buying presents for his children. But fate was cruel; he was suddenly seized with a heart attack and died. Clenching the telegram notifying them of the death of his father, little Kiyoharu, then a sixth grade pupil in elementary school, crossed the Tsugaru Strait from Aomori to Hakodate on a ferry with his mother, Kyo, now 54 and a member of the guidance staff of a Soka Gakkai district organization. Kiyoharu still remembers his mother bursting into tears, as she embraced the plain square box containing her husband's ashes.

The Ogasawaras were a prestigious family, their ancestors being one of the first to settle in the area and open up the fishing port of Shitsukari. In particular, their house served as the lodging place for the traveling blind women shamans, known as itako, for which Aomori Prefecture is noted.

Having lost her husband, Mrs. Ogasawara now had to raise her four children all alone, the oldest child being 12 year old Kiyoharu. She also made regular visits to the hospital where her second son Hisao was hospitalized. By foot and then by bus, it took her two hours to the hospital in Mutsu City. At times, she grumbled about her fate, about why there was no end to the misfortunes despite the fact that the family was so religious from the time of its ancestors. A nurse at the hospital, who couldn't bear to see her in such distress, tried to encourage and comfort her as much as possible. She began handing Mrs. Ogasawara clippings from the Soka Gakkai newspaper the Seikyo Shimbun containing accounts of Soka Gakkai members who overcame their misfortunes and sufferings through the practice of their Buddhist faith. Mrs. Ogasawara read them eagerly, for she, too, was filled with the strong desire to see her son well again. As she continued to read the newspaper, she was moved by the scientific nature of the religion, much different from the shamanism she was accustomed to. In February, 1963, the entire family joined the Soka Gakkai and took up faith in Nichiren Shoshu. The village was steeped in time-honored customs and tradition, and naturally, the family was subject to harsh criticism by the relatives and villagers for changing religion. However, the criticism died down about half a year later when the grandfather joined Soka Gakkai.

Being in the depths of poverty, the family sold the household effects to make both ends meet. Heartrending as it was, it also had to part with the fishing boat, so essential to a fishing family. Young Kiyoharu tightly clung to the boat as people came to take it away.

Gradually, the second son's condition began to improve and he passed the critical stage. Soon, he was able to leave the hospital.

It was a trying period for both Kiyoharu and the family, but he was thankful to his mother for giving him the chance to study at high school. He was thankful also to Soka Gakkai whose members continued to encourage him and give him confidence. The mother actively participated in Soka Gakkai activities after work and visited outlying villages to tell others of the benefits of her Buddhist faith.

The article goes on to tell how Kiyoharu, after graduating from high school, joined a fishing cooperative where he engaged in extensive research about fishing methods. Discovering a novel way to catch a squid, he quit his job, bought a fishing boat and was brilliantly successful as a fisherman. He told his secret to others in the village and everybody prospered as never before. He became head of the local fishery research association and of the local PTA. In addition he devoted many of his evenings to Soka Gakkai activities. The article concludes:

> The Ogasawara family had challenged its problems and, through deep faith in Nichiren Daishonin's Buddhism, had established a peaceful and harmonious household, contributing to the happiness and welfare of the community.[6]

The essay contains all of the elements of why new members say they join the Soka Gakkai. The Ogasawara family suffered from illness, death, poverty, and despair. At the most difficult time of her life, Mrs. Ogasawara was consoled by a Gakkai member and was told that by turning to this form of Buddhism her troubles would be over. In desperation, she followed this advice and had her whole family join. Things did not improve immediately, but the family gained a sense of confidence, worked hard and, in the end, flourished.

Remaining a member of the Soka Gakkai, however, means ongoing commitment. The new member is told that further gain without renewed faith and practice is impossible. Any lapse of activity will lead to a return of bad karma and misfortune. Therefore, it is imperative for the member to keep up all phases of the daily religious practice.

The interviews and newspaper experience detailed above involved people who have found success through Soka Gakkai membership. Any Soka Gakkai official or member will readily admit that there are some--but not many--cases where converts do not find satisfaction through membership and abandon the faith. When people fail, the Gakkai says that they failed because their faith was not deep enough or that they did not practice hard enough.

The happy member is convinced that somehow he has received great favors from the gohonzon. This leads to a sense of gratitude and dedication. More importantly, it seems to give him a sense of confidence that may not have been there before. One success leads to another, and setbacks only strengthen the determination to succeed.

How seriously can one take Soka Gakkai claims concerning the benefits it offers members? As a scholar and nonmember, I cannot discuss these claims in religious terms. It is what the member believes that is important. For those with financial problems or mild emotional problems, friendship and encouragement from other Soka Gakkai members can mean a great deal. Being told that prayer and proselytization can lead to greater self-confidence and other benefits can make the sufferer work hard and have a feeling of achievement. Thus, in these areas, Soka Gakkai membership can have positive effects. It is the area of medical claims that causes problems for many nonmembers.

A western observer might well be disturbed by the claims of medical progress through prayer. A Westerner has probably heard of successful cases of faith healing in Christianity, but most people in the West, as in Japan, rely on modern science and medicine for cures. Soka Gakkai members and documents often imply that the ultimate cause of disease is related to bad karma and that the ultimate cure can only come from cleansing the karma. Members who are ill, however, are urged to see doctors, as well as to pray. Chanting and proselytization may help to remove the underlying causes of a medical problem, but doctors are necessary to help the process along.

Nevertheless, there is a certain danger in the Gakkai's views on the cause and treatment of illness. Very often physical or emotional problems are so serious that they require professional attention. If a follower is convinced that Nichiren Shoshu can really cure his illness or solve his problems, he may well ignore help from the doctor or psychiatrist who really could help him. I have heard of cases where ill people joined the Gakkai hoping to find a cure and who became even more ill or died because they did not seek medical help.

It is interesting to note that American members of the Soka Gakkai's chapter in the United States, the Nichiren Shoshu Soka Gakkai of America (NSA), join the NSA for many of the same reasons as their Japanese counterparts. In his book, Umi o Watatta Nihon Shukyo[7], Inoue Nobutaka describes the average American member as a person who is slightly alienated from society, who is seeking meaning in life, and who has experienced failure or frustrations in his career and/or marriage. NSA apparently provides these people with a sense of direction, a chance to discuss their problems with other like-minded people, and a set of beliefs that they lacked previously. The main difference between American and Japanese members is that Americans do not usually join because of physical problems.

# NOTES

[1]Interview with Soka Gakkai President Akiya in Tokyo, 20 March 1987.

[2]Ibid.

[3]White, p. 85.

[4]White, pp. 85-86.

[5]In a survey conducted in 1967 by the Soka Gakkai and reported in the Seikyo Shimbun, respondents gave the following responses to the question, "What problem did you have before you joined?"

> Anxiety about the future = 46%
> Lack of friends = 34%
> Financial difficulties = 20%
> Ill health = 15%
> Family Discord = 15%
> Other = 14%

Murata Kiyoaki in his book Japan's New Buddhism writes:

"Had a similar survey been conducted 10 years earlier, the percentages for financial difficulties and ill health would probably have been higher. The 1967 figures suggest that a change has occurred, in the last decade, in the social strata from which Soka Gakkai draws its members. The poll also reflects the social and economic changes that have taken place in Japan over the same period."

See Murata Kiyoaki, Japan's New Buddhism (Tokyo, 1969), p. 159.

[6]Quoted from the Soka Gakkai News (September, 1984), pp. 12-15. The article was translated directly from an earlier issue of the Seikyo Shimbun.

[7]Inoue Nobutaka, Umi o Watatta Nihon Shukyo (Tokyo, 1985).

# CHAPTER 5

## CITIZENS OF THE PROMISED LAND:
## A PERSONALITY PROFILE OF SOKA GAKKAI MEMBERS

The Soka Gakkai in its eschatological liturgy promises a world of creative Buddhas who will bring on a new realm of peace, love, and creativity. People with mundane and unhappy backgrounds will become dedicated, successful, and creative leaders. Their suffering will be at an end, and they can look forward to happy and meaningful lives.

Today when analyzing the Soka Gakkai, one will find two camps. Nonmembers are still somewhat hostile to the Soka Gakkai and have a generally negative view of the movement's leaders, while Gakkai followers are very enthusiastic about the Gakkai and its leadership. To understand the Gakkai and what kinds of people accept its message, one must take a look at its membership.

A Japanese political scientist writing about the Soka Gakkai in the late 1950s noted that the Gakkai recruited its members mainly from the uneducated, lower-income group, which includes many unskilled manual workers; only a token number of intellectuals and higher income people were members.[1] Today the average Japanese is much better educated, a good deal wealthier, and older than his counterpart a generation ago. There is every indication that such demographic trends have occurred within the Gakkai as well.

The actual size of the Soka Gakkai has always been a matter of dispute. Some political scientists in Japan speculate that the actual active membership may be as low as one or two million households, while Soka Gakkai officials have consistently put their membership at about seven million households or ten million people, slightly less than ten percent of the overall population of Japan.[2] Figures compiled by the Japanese government in 1985 found 16,887,728 Nichiren Shoshu adherents.[3] These figures, however, are suspect for the simple fact that they list 220,694,145 followers of religious sects in a nation with a hundred million fewer people.

Another way of gauging membership is by studying voting trends of the Komeito in local and national elections. In the 1970s, there was a very close correlation between the number of votes the Komeito received in national elections and estimated Gakkai membership levels. It is a widely held assumption among Japanese political scientists that roughly ninety percent of Soka Gakkai members who vote support the Komeito and that support for the Komeito outside of the Soka Gakkai is fairly small. For example, in a 1984 survey conducted among one hundred Waseda University students, none of whom belonged to the Gakkai, only four students said that they would even consider the possibility of voting for the komeito. During that period sharp rises or declines in Gakkai membership were followed two years later by a similar rise or decline in the Komeito vote. Thus, the Fjiwara scandal of 1970 led to a quick but temporary decline in membership. There were subsequent Komeito reverses in the 1971 and 1972 national elections. Gakkai membership reached its nadir in early 1971 and quickly rose to previous heights. This trend was reflected in the Komeito's improved performances in the 1973 and 1977 Tokyo Municipal Assembly elections, in the Upper House elections of 1974 and 1977, and the Lower House contest of 1976.[4] In Lower House elections between 1972 and 1983, the Komeito received about ten percent of the total vote and 6.6 percent of the total eligible vote.[5] A variety of other surveys taken in the early 1970s indicated that three-quarters of the Komeito vote came from Soka Gakkai members, and there is nothing to show that this trend is not continuing. Based on this data, one can speculate that the Soka Gakkai has the support of about six to eight percent of the total population, though it is much harder to say how many of these people are in fact active members.

In his study of the Soka Gakkai in the late 1960s, James White[6] found that the Gakkai was a middle-aged group only slightly younger than the nation as a whole. White found that the Gakkai had a relatively little-educated membership, though the few well-educated members held a disproportionately large number of the leadership positions. White states that the Gakkai was predominantly an urban phenomenon and that although the Gakkai claimed to be a microcosm of Japanese society, housewives and laborers were extraordinarily numerous while official, managerial, professional, and technical personnel, white-collar workers, students, and persons engaged in agriculture, forestry, and fishing were rare.[7] White found that people engaged in medium to small-scale and self-owned commercial and industrial enterprises, especially shops, and in sales and services of all kinds were also somewhat overrepresented when compared to a nationwide sample of professions.[8]

In terms of political activity, White was unable to determine what the voting behavior of members had been prior to their conversion; he presumed that the Gakkai had been attracting people who were previously politically inactive. He discovered that possibly one aspect of Soka Gakkai membership was a vast amount of politicization; in one sample ninety-eight percent of a small sample of adult members reported voting in an Upper House election.[9]

80

White defined the characteristics of the model member of the Gakkai:

> [She is] (1) a woman who (2) is in her thirties or forties, (3) has less than a high school education, (4) lives in the city, (5) is a housewife, (if a man, he is a laborer or is engaged in some commercial or service enterprise, (6) receives a family income of 40,000 yen (111) a month or less, (7) was brought into the Gakkai by a relative or neighbor, (if a man, possibly by a friend or co-worker), (8) was motivated to join primarily by problems of mental or social conflict and secondarily by problems of economics and health, and (9) was to a certain degree unconcerned with any specific Gakkai doctrines.

> The activist element in the Society differs from the general membership in several respects. The typical activist is (1) a man who (2) is in his twenties or thirties, (3) is much more likely to have a high school or college education--though nine years or less is still modal, (4) also still lives in the city, (5) is a laborer or is engaged in some commercial or service enterprise and is not a member of any trade union, and (6) earns between 50,000 and 70,000 yen ($140-195) a month. [10]

Conditions in Japan in the mid-1980s are much different than they were two decades ago. Today every segment of Japanese society has shared in the economic boom to some extent. While I was doing research on the Soka Gakkai in the summers of 1984 and 1985, I met no member who was suffering greatly from economic want and who felt that he was not sharing in the new-found affluence. On the other hand, while many of the members interviewed had enough money to meet their very basic needs and comforts, they did not have the resources to afford some of the luxuries that wealthier Japanese are more accustomed to. In other words, the kind of person that the Soka Gakkai might have appealed to in the 1960s is less common today.

I attended three neighborhood meetings in 1984 in Tokyo and Kawasaki. One meeting was in a fairly upperclass area of Tokyo (Ota Ward) and the two others were in nondescript middle-class areas. While these figures may not be typical of the movement of the whole, one could see the following based on a sample of about 150 people who attended the meetings:

Males: 55%        Females: 45%

Young (up to about age 25): 30%

Middle Aged (25-55 years old): 50%

Over age 55: 20%

Various Soka Gakkai officials stated that in terms of overall membership, women outnumber men by a small number, but to call the Soka Gakkai largely a female-based movement would be a grave mistake. A glance at any large general mass meeting will reveal that the Soka Gakkai is no longer a movement of the young; instead it is a grouping of middle-aged people in their later thirties and forties with a healthy number of younger and older people. When I gave presentations before Soka Gakkai groups ranging in size from a small group of thirty to a mass gathering of five thousand, I got the strong impression that the average person in the audience was five to ten years older than I. (I was 35 at the time.)

One gets the impression that while housewives and blue collar workers still form a significant part of the Soka Gakkai membership, the occupational level and occupational achievements are much higher than they were in the 1960s. This partly reflects a strong national trend that has led to more and better quality education for the population as a whole and a decrease in the number of people in the primary and secondary sectors of the economy. However, the Soka Gakkai itself is also responsible for this membership shift. Today the Soka Gakkai, with its own excellent school system and its political, educational, and economic successes, attracts many well-educated and articulate leaders and members. In 1984, at various colleges I was introduced to several hundred young scholars, teachers, and students who were active in the Soka Gakkai. While these kinds of people are still in the minority, they are far better represented than they were a generation ago. It is also clear that members have ample opportunities to improve on their education. All members are encouraged to read organizational newspapers and magazines in addition to the Gosho (sacred literature) and to pass written exams to demonstrate their learning. This reading and training for exams provides members with some additional schooling. For each community meeting members are supposed to have read a portion of the Gosho and other inspirational literature, which can only help their reading ability.

Thus, in summary, it is safe to say that the Soka Gakkai still holds the allegiance of a significant portion of the Japanese population, although there is no indication that the Gakkai is growing as it did in the 1960s and early 1970s. A hint of this is the steadiness of the total Komeito vote. In elections with a low voter turn-out, the Komeito will do very well, as it did in 1983. The 1983 election was on a cold and rainy day and many voters stayed away, but highly politicized Gakkai members voted en masse. In the previous election, however, there were two elections on the same day--for both Houses of the Diet. The result was that while the Komeito vote stayed constant, the party lost a great many seats because a great number of voters supported other parties. There was a similar result in the 1986 elections in which the Komeito was the only party to hold its own.

In recent years attitudes toward the Soka Gakkai have changed. My own surveys indicate that members are highly enthusiastic about the organization and give strong support to its leaders, and today the Gakkai is older, quieter, and more a part of the establishment than in the late 1960s. The harsh antagonism that one found among so many Japanese a generation ago vis-a-vis the Soka Gakkai has diminished greatly. By separating itself from active political activities, eliminating the caustic proselytization (shakubuku) methods of the past, and working hard to support peace and the current constitution, the Soka Gakkai is much less controversial than in the past and its public image is far more positive.

The Gakkai remains largely an urban phenomenon with notable strength in the Kanto and Kansai regions and in Fukuoka, but there are significant chapters in every prefecture, even in the most remote rural regions. The Gakkai still attracts a healthy number of young people, but the typical member today is a person in his or her late thirties or early forties with at least a high school education--and very often some work in college as well--with an average income. I have met representatives from virtually every major profession; but housewives, self-employed people in various fields of commerce, and middle level kaisha-in (white-collar employee at a large Japanese company) constitute the largest number of Gakkai members.

## Two Soka Gakkai Families

An analysis of two Japanese families with Soka Gakkai members will give a clearer picture of the lives of the average family. The first family is unified in its devotion to Nichiren Shoshu Buddhism and the Gakkai movement, while the second is divided in its support. One will find examples of both kinds of families in Japan.

A Family United:

    This family consists of a father and mother in their late thirties who live with their two small children in a two-room apartment in a danchi (large apartment buildings that surround Tokyo) in one of the outlying wards of Tokyo. The father is from Osaka and is from a middle-class family that put a premium on education for its children. His brother, together with other family members, runs a successful small sushi restaurant in Osaka. The father went to Tokyo after graduating from one of the better colleges in the Osaka area. Today he is a successful member of the managerial staff of a large Tokyo company.

    The father's parents joined the Soka Gakkai in its early days and have remained loyal members to this day. All of their children are also avid members of the Gakkai movement. The father met his wife, also a Soka Gakkai member, at the company where they were both employed. Both remain deeply committed to the Soka Gakkai and devote most of their spare time to Soka Gakkai activities. The wife is a member of the Women's Division and is one of the leaders in her district. The father belongs to various Soka Gakkai organizations and often lectures about the teachings of Nichiren Shoshu at meetings. In their apartment, a gohonzon occupies the place of greatest honor. The family actively engages in every aspect of the daily life of a member as described below and socializes mainly with other Gakkai members.

A Family Divided:

    This family's economic and social status is very typical of the improvements in the quality of life that have occurred in Japan since World War II. The family today lives comfortably in a small house in an industrial city near Tokyo. The household consists of a father and mother in their early sixties, two sons, and a daughter.

The father has worked as an engineer in a small construction company for over thirty years and makes a comfortable living. His family owns its own home and enjoys many of the basic luxuries of life, including the most modern camera and television equipment. The father and mother never went to college but have put a premium on education for their children, all of whom went to college. The daughter is married to a successful kaisha-in. The eldest son is a music teacher and lives with his wife and two children in a tiny house only a few meters away from his parents' home. The parents saved enough money to send their youngest son to a small American college for a year. He did brilliantly in school and is now preparing to become an English teacher in the secondary school.

The maternal grandparents were among the original members of the Soka Gakkai, joining the organization in the late 1940s. They have remained devout followers. Their daughter is not an active member of the Soka Gakkai, but she is a strong supporter of the movement and its beliefs. Her daughter is likewise a strong supporter of the movement and the two sons are sympathetic, though not practicing members.

The conflict comes with the outspoken hatred for the movement from the father. He is convinced that the Soka Gakkai is a fraudulent movement taking money from gullible people with false promises of happiness. He believes that the motives of the Gakkai leaders are to achieve political power and accumulate great wealth at the expense of believers, who will follow every command from above. He is uncomfortable even talking about the Gakkai and takes every opportunity to denounce it.

The father's antagonism causes a real split in the family, which is in every other way very loving and close. The supporters of the Gakkai refuse to give up their beliefs but suppress their feelings to avoid conflict with the father. They are not openly members of the Gakkai and do not attend Gakkai meetings in their neighborhood, but they vote for Komeito canidates in elections and remain sympathetic to the Gakkai. There is no real anger at the father for his views; rather, the children and mother never bring up the issue with him and continue to follow their beliefs quietly in the background.

The Soka Gakkai View of Ideal Members:

The Soka Gakkai relies on testimonies of devout members to demonstrate the strengths of its religious beliefs. One will find "Experiences" in virtually every Soka Gakkai publication--articles written by Gakkai reporters about the lives of various members. The following profile of Professor Yamaki Setsuo as an ideal member was featured in a recent article in the Seikyo Shimbun.

Professor Yamaki Setsuo is a senior professor of economics at Toyo University in Tokyo. He comes from a lower-middle class background. His father operated a not very successful liquor store and was a violent alcoholic. Fortunately, Yamaki Setsuo was urged on by his mother, who said, "You will only become an ordinary man if you only exert ordinary efforts. You must make an outstanding achievement if you are to become a superior man." Determined to succeed where his father had not, he studied hard. While a graduate student at Chuo University in Tokyo, a fellow student who was a Soka Gakkai member urged him to attend a Gakkai meeting. He went and was intellectually interested enough in the form of Buddhism being discussed there to join, but he was not a fervent member. His wife had joined the Soka Gakkai in high school but had generally abandoned her practice, and it was long after their engagement that he found out that she was at least technically a member. According to the Seikyo Shimbun:

> Soon, his wife became pregnant, and Mr. Yamaki became uneasy. He thought, `There's no guarantee that I would become successful as a scholar. Could I support my family?' As he became uncertain about himself, he changed and listened to the guidance of a senior member of the Young Men's Division. Mr. Yamaki read many Soka Gakkai publications. One of them was a book by then Soka Gakkai President Daisaku Ikeda...about religion and politics. He was greatly impressed by President Ikeda's words that true equality and freedom can only be materialized if there is respect for the dignity of human life. Mr. Yamaki well knew that freedom and equality on materialistic dimensions were not true freedom and equality. He felt that through Ikeda's book, he had come in contact with a profound thought.

> Mr. Yamaki was aroused: `Learning without humanity in mind is like a house built on sand.' Awakened, he visited a senior member of the Soka Gakkai and told him that he would do the Buddhist prayers seriously and develop his faith. That was in February, 1970. A complete change came over him. He said to himself, `As long as I am going to devote myself to faith, I might as well go all out.' He offered to deliver the Seikyo Shimbun every day. He faithfully did his prayers and he never failed to attend meetings. Moved by her husband's actions, Mrs. Yamaki followed suit.

Yamaki got his first teaching job in April, 1970 and soon thereafter received his Ph.D. in economics. He was determined to become a famous scholar, but a friend cautioned him, noting:

> Mr. Yamaki absorbed himself in his studies not because of a keen interest in the field of learning. It was because he wanted fame and a name for himself by becoming a professor. Consequently, he did not enjoy studying; it was more of a pain. It was only

after he had awakened to the Buddhist faith that he felt true joy in his pursuit. He had concluded that learning, after all, boils down to a `study of humanity.' Leaning for him became a mission to contribute to society.

When he was young, he was very timid and reluctant to speak to people. Although he aspired to become a teacher, he was always concerned about his weakness; he felt a sense of fulfillment and developed a strong life force. His pursuit was greatly stimulated by Buddhism, and in 1974 he was promoted to become assistant professor, only two years after he had become professor.

Yamaki advanced in his field, translated a book from German with success, and in 1978 became a professor and then dean at Toyo University in Tokyo.

(In 1979) Tokyo was rocked by campus disputes which had spread nationwide. (Dean) Yamaki was compelled to hold mass bargaining sessions with the students. At times, he was detained until late at night. The other professors, who ordinarily were tolerant with the students, took an uncompromising stand and warned Mr. Yamaki not to regard students as being sensible and intelligent.

Mr. Yamaki, however, persisted in talking to the students. He realized that the root cause of the dispute was the gap in thought between students and professors, and held the strong conviction that both the teachers and learners should establish a relationship on equal footing. The students became more violent in pressing their demands, and many professors criticized Mr. Yamaki for being too lenient in tolerating the demands of the students. Despite the criticism Mr. Yamaki believes that a university is a place to develop human beings, that the acquirement of advanced specialized knowledge is fruitless unless there is a development of humanity...

Mr. Yamaki always admonishes himself with the educational philosophy of Soka Gakkai's founder and first president, Mr. Tsunesaburo Makiguchi: `Life without learning is like groping in the dark; learning isolated from daily life is empty.'[11]

Becoming a Member:

Becoming a member of the Soka Gakkai means the joining of a new religion--Nichiren Shoshu--and the abandonment of all old religious ties.  After a person has been contracted by a Soka Gakkai member and expresses some interest in the movement, he must go through a five-step process.

The first step is to accompany his Soka Gakkai mentor to one of the monthly discussion meetings (zadankai).  At the meeting he listens to the testimonies given by members and lectures by Soka Gakkai leaders.  At each meeting that I attended, the prospective member was introduced and was asked a variety of questions by members present.

The second step for the person who decides to pursue the entry process is to consult his family.  Soka Gakkai officials explain that this step is crucial because membership means a renunciation of all former religious ties.  The member that accompanied him to the discussion meeting must also visit the person's home to meet with his family to discuss the implications of membership.

The third step is for the prospective member to remove from his home all religious objects of worship, including small Buddhist altars and Shinto shrines found in so many Japanese homes.  The Soka Gakkai is firm on this point.  According to one Gakkai publication:

> Is it not permissible to keep sacred objects and tablets of other religions without burning them as long as one does not worship them?  The answer is: Nichiren Daishonin pointed out that the cause of unhappiness is evil religion.  Wanting to keep relics of other religions on the pretext that you don't worship them indicates your attachment to evil

religions. Then you can't say that your faith is unadulterated. There are cases of people who mistakenly thought that they had disposed of tablets and talismans of evil religions. Because these objects remained in their homes, however, these people suffered severe divine punishment.... If you decide to join our faith after realizing that Nichiren Shoshu is correct and that all other religions are evil, then it is natural for you to carry out hobobarai (removal of evil religion).[12]

The fourth step is a visit to a nearby Nichiren Shoshu temple either in the company of the person who introduced him to the faith or with other senior Soka Gakkai officials. There is a brief ceremony performed by the priest at which the new member receives the gohonzon and vows to cherish it forever. The fifth step is accomplished when the new member takes the gohonzon home and places it in his family altar. Then starts the daily ritual of morning and evening prayer which is central to the belief and practice of any member.

Daily Life of the Soka Gakkai Member

Membership in the Soka Gakkai is not an all-consuming activity. Unlike some religious cults that demand the total time and dedication of a member which alienates him from the mainstream of society, the Soka Gakkai, like other traditional religious groups, seeks to improve the life of the person in society. The member carries on a normal life at home and at work, but the Soka Gakkai expects the true believer to devote a significant amount of his time to Gakkai-related activities. Normal activities include gongyo or daily prayer, attendance at various neighborhood meetings (zadankai) that are usually held on a monthly basis, the study of the basic teachings of Nichiren Shoshu (syogaku), shakubuku or proselythzation,and pilgrimages (tozan) to Taiseki-ji.

Gongyo: Gongyo is the most basic and important practice of any Soka Gakkai member. Literally, it means "assiduous practice" and is the recital of Buddhist sutras in front of an object of worship. In Nichiren Shoshu, gongyo means chanting "Nam-Myoho-Renge-Kyo" and reciting part of the Hoben (second) chapter and the entire Juryo (sixteenth) chapter of the Lotus Sutra in front of the gohonzon. A follower is supposed to spend a minimum of a few minutes a day performing the gongyo.

Zadankai: The Zadankai are monthly neighborhood meetings that play important educational and socialization roles for the members. They provide members of a given area the opportunity to meet and to gain a sense of solidarity. In general, worship is done in the privacy of one's home; one rarely goes to a public worship service, especially in one's own neighborhood with other believers. Thus, the average Gakkai member is robbed of the critical socialization process found in Christian churches where members of the same congregation meet to worship on a regular basis once a week. The zadankai provide the member with the chance to meet other members in his neighborhood, to communicate with them at length, to hear lectures and learn from Gakkai leaders, and, most importantly, to pray together.[13] According to one Gakkai official, the purpose of the zadankai is to give members a chance to discuss Buddhism informally and thereby deepen faith. Another is to acquaint prospective members with Buddhism's grandeur. It brings people from a certain community together and creates a sense of unity that superceded differences in age, education, sex, work, etc.[14]

The zadankai are structured, but not excessively. Each agenda is established by Gakkai leaders along general guidelines for the month's activities, but there is considerable flexibility as to what goes on in each meeting and a considerable amount of autonomy as to the planning of more minute details. Members will study the same passages from the Gosho across Japan at zadankai. A typical program consists of songs, a group gongyo, official announcement, short explanations of articles of faith, the skakubuku of visitors, discussion of common problems in light of scripture, personal testimonials of faith, and the like.

I attended several zadankai in June, 1984 in Tokyo. Each was held in the home of a member. One district meeting attracted about fifty people from the surrounding neighborhood. It started off with the performance of the gongyo followed by two songs, the Soka Gakkai song "Kofu ni hashire" (Advance toward kosen-rufu) and a chorus by young members of the Future Division who sang "Bokura no chikai" (Our Oath). A member then gave a graphic lecture on the concept of the Ten Worlds using cartoons to denote the horrors of hell in life and the bliss of Buddhahood. ([Jukai] The ten life conditions ranging from a hellish nature to the purity of Buddhahood that every person can experience in life [Source: Nichiren Shoshu Kyogaku Shojiten (Tokyo, 1974.], p. 184.)

Three members then got up to tell personal experiences which led either to membership or a renewal of faith. An elderly man got up to say that he had experienced a severe blood pressure problem the preceding year. A Gakkai member suggested fervent chanting and frequent gongyo sessions. He did so and notes, "As you can see, I am in good health for my age. It is a strong testimony to the strength of faith and practice." A young housewife and mother of two small children said that her husband's low salary and mounting debts made it necessary for her to go to work at once. Her local ward office, however, told her that she would have to wait a long time for a place in the local daycare center and that if she returned to work, her family's income would be too high to qualify for placement in the center.

Faced with a real dilemma and in a great state of depression, a Gakkai member suggested active gongyo and shakubuku. She agreed, and to her amazement within a week a letter form the ward office informed her that there were places for both of her children and that she could go to work without penalty. A youngish man got up to say that he had lived near Nagoya and had made a good living in the area's old textile industry. When the industry collapsed in the 1970s, he was without a job and in extreme depression. In despair, he turned to the gohonzon and chanted fervently. In rapid succession he got another good job and then put together funds to buy a small supermarket. "Look outside the window and you can see my store with all its customers and bright lights."

Following the introduction of a new member who stated he had been an atheist all his life and was now happy for the first time, there was a lecture by a leader of the Gakkai's Women's Division, who told of the hope and encouragement President Toda gave her and other women in 1951 when the Division was first formed. The District Leader then gave a lecture based on the Gosho for the month and on the implications of its teachings.

The zadankai are vital because they provide members with a sense of solidarity. They also serve as a justification for the hard work and time that Gakkai membership brings because members are given proof positive that success and happiness can come through membership. The mood of the meetings is upbeat and positive. Everybody who speaks is successful, and there is never a sign of failure. There is no criticism or harsh words. James White is correct when he likens the zadankai to group therapy as opposed to brain-washing, where self-criticism is often found.[15] Another often successful feature is the group shakubuku of

94

nonmember guests. Members often invite friends or colleagues to the meetings with the purpose of seeing "proof" of the success of true faith.[16]

Kyogaku: The Soka Gakkai places a premium on the study of the basic teachings of its faith. There are frequent study sessions, and vast amounts of material are distributed or sold to members. According to one Gakkai official, "Study is important to broaden the member's base of knowledge of Buddhist philosophy. The knowledge that the believer receives deepens his faith and serves as a well-spring of values."[17]

Members make the study of Nichiren's writings a central part of their lives. Gakkai members are supposed to attend special study sessions which are held every other month. In addition, there are lectures and discussions on the Gosho writings at the monthly zadankai.

To encourage leaning, the Gakkai's Study Department gives a series of exams at regular intervals to members. People who pass the series of exams, which start at a very elementary level and terminate at a high and very difficult stage, are given one of six titles ranging from assistant lecturer to full professor. These ranks are mainly for prestige purposes--the vast majority of people who pass the exams are not given any paying jobs or special responsibilities, although the few people with the rank of professor are permitted to give occasional lectures at zadankai.[18]

Shakubuku: Propagation of the faith is a very important activity. According to tradition, shakubuku is regarded as a method of refuting another's attachment to what the believer feels are the other's "heretical views." According to Ikeda Daisaku:

> If one asks why we must do shakubuku, it is because
> we receive merit and become Buddhas by doing it.
> In everyday life if we don't do what the boss asks,

then we won't get paid. We will be fired! It is a wrong. It is quite reasonable that if we don't work, we will not get paid. No matter if we are sleepy or if it's hot or cold out, in order to receive a decent salary or some merit, we must follow our boss' commands and also our Master's guidelines. By doing so we can live without worry.

Nichiren Daishonin taught that the practice of becoming a Buddha in mappo involves individual practice and conversion of others. This involves chanting the daimoku and doing shakubuku and without the daimoku and shakubuku, nothing can or will happen. This is the only practice in mappo. [19]

The Soka Gakkai developed a bad reputation among nonbelievers in the 1950s and 1960s because of the fanatical attempts of some avid members almost to force others to become members. Some of my older American and Japanese friends recount how in the early days of the Gakkai they were approached by members and constantly harangued about the benefits of membership. One American had a Japanese neighbor who was a member of the Soka Gakkai. The neighbor bothered the American day and night until the American finally moved out in frustration. Members considered it a sacred duty to convert as many people as possible, even if undue pressure had to be applied.

Today this public and pressurized form of shakubuku has been largely, if not entirely, abandoned. Rather, the approach now is quite subtle. When talking to members, one finds a recurrent theme. At one time in the past each member was facing some great personal crisis and was very unhappy with life. A Soka Gakkai member then approached the distressed person, offered him a few words of consolation, and told him about this wonderful new religion that would help him solve his problems. I have found, however, that in other everyday relationships nonmembers are rarely harassed by member co-workers.

Tozan: Making pilgimages to Taiseki-ji is an important activity for many members. Taiseki-ji, an old temple, was founded in 1290 by Nikko Shonin, the second high priest of Nichiren Shoshu. It has been the head temple of the sect since that date. For many years it was a very small temple located under Mount Fuji, but it has exploded in size with the postwar expansion of the Soka Gakkai. Dozen of modern buildings have been added, including dormitories, meeting and reception halls, and the majestic Sho-Hondo (Grand Main Temple) completed in 1972. It seems almost as big as a domed baseball stadium. The Daigohonzon is kept in the building, and it is the most sacred place of worship for followers of Nichiren Shoshu.

The primary object of the pilgrimage is to worship the Daigohonzon. Every member has a gohonzon in his home, but it is much more efficacious to pray before the real thing. A visit also gives the member a strong impression of the strength and grandeur of the movement. Upon entering the temple compound, a visitor walks down long wide paths flanked on either side by beautiful gardens, fountains, huge modern buildings, and trees and buildings that are centuries old. The climax of the visit is to wait outside the Sho Hondo next to its immense fountain, columns, and soaring white walls. Going in with thousands of people gives a member the strong impression that he does belong to a huge movement.

Other ongoing activities at Taiseki-ji included large study sessions, talks by visiting Gakkai dignitaries, festivals, and exhibits of various kinds.

Other Activities:

There are also a wide variety of ad hoc activities that play an important role in a member's life. Many, if not most, members ts belong to one of the divisions of the Soka Gakkai. An important feature of Soka Gakkai life is the Cultural Festival. Festivities are held both on a national basis at such places as Hiroshima or Taiseki-ji, or on a regional or prefectural basis. These festivals have a lot of "folk-oriented" acts including guymnasitcs, dances, and song sessions involving hundreds of people. Sometimes it seems that there are as many performers as people in the audience. Preparation takes a great deal of time for the many people who choose to be involved in the folk festival. Members are also asked to attend public lectures, go to Gakkai-sponsored exhibitions, and perhaps raise money for African relief and the like.

Soka Gakkai Membership and the Future:

There is every indication that the Soka Gakkai will continue to thrive. Membership figures should remain fairly constant, but members will become older because of demographic trends in Japan. Members will probably continue to have the same economic and educational background as they do now.

# NOTES

[1]Watanuki Joji, _Politics in Postwar Japanese Society_ (Tokyo, 1977), p. 84.

[2]Interview with Yamaguchi Hiromu, International Office of the Soka Gakkai, on 20 March 1987 in Tokyo.

[3]_Asahi Nenkan_ (1986), p. 854.

[4]The following figures seem to support this thesis:

Estimated Membership (in millions)

| | |
|---|---|
| 1962 - 4.2 | 1965 - 4.8 |
| 1968 - 6.5 | 1970 - 7.5 |
| 1972 - 6.2 | 1974 - 6.9 |
| 1976 - 8.0 | |

Komeito Upper House Performance

1962 - 4.1
1965 - 5.1
1968 - 6.6
1971 - 5.6
1974 - 6.4
1977 - 7.1

[5]Arai Kunio, "Why the Liberal Democrats Barely Survived." in the _Japan Echo_, XI.2 (Summer, 1984), p. 11.

[6]James White, _The Soka Gakkai and Mass Society_ (Stanford, 1970).

[7]Ibid., p. 69.

[8]Ibid., p. 72.

[9]Ibid., p. 75.

[10]Ibid., p. 76.

[11]Quoted from the _Seikyo Shimbun_ in the _Soka Gakkai News_ (January 1985), pp. 15-19.

[12]Kodaira Yoshiehei, Soka Gakkai (Tokyo, 1962), p. 140 quoted from Kurata Kiyoaki, Japan's New Buddhism (Tokyo, 1969), p. 106.

[13]A Dictionary of Buddhist Terms and Concepts (Tokyo, 1983), p. 145.

[14]Interview with Harashima Tzkashi (Soka Gakkai Study Department) July 25, 1984.

[15]White, p. 91.

[16]Interview with Yamaguchi Hiromu (Soka Gakkai Official), June 1984.

[17]Interview with Shiotsu Tohru (Soka Gakkai Official), in Tokyo, June 19, 1984.

[18]Ibid.

[19]Quoted in Kasahara Kazuo, Tenkanki no Shukyo (Tokyo, 1974), p. 271.

# CHAPTER 6

## JAPANESE BUDDHISM IN THE UNITED STATES:
### The Surprising Success of the Nichiren Shoshu of America

The Soka Gakkai stresses in its eschatological messages that even if Japan were to become a Buddhaland full of enlightened citizenry, the rest of the world would still be living in a more depraved state. A Russian missile set to the United States or an American nuclear strike against Russia could destroy the whole world. Thus, in order to safeguard Nichiren's message and to bring peace and happiness to all mankind, the Gakkai is convinced that Nichiren Shoshu's message must be sent abroad.

The Soka Gakkai believes that Nichiren Shoshu must be a global religion and has made a strong effort to spread its Buddhism throughout the world. The Gakkai explains that this effort "was in fact the Daishonin's intention. Nichiren Shoshu is a world religion with the power to bring peace and happiness everywhere."[1] According to Soka Gakkai figures, there are chapters in at least 115 countries and about one and a quarter million believers outside of Japan. There are also seven temples, sixty-four community centers, and three training centers abroad. The largest concentrations of members are in the United States (500,000 believers)[2] and Brazil (108,000 believers).[3]

Nichiren Shoshu organizations are at least technically independent of the headquarters in Japan and many foreign chapters have incorporated locally. The Soka Gakkai coordinates its international activities through two bodies centered in Tokyo: Soka Gakkai International (SGI) and the Nichiren Shoshu International Center (NSIC). SGI is not a formal body or bureau as such; rather it is the symbolic name given to the whole international movement and means the same thing to the Gakkai that the concept of a world church or body of Christ might mean to some Christians. The Soka Gakkai gives Ikeda Daisaku the title of President of SGI though, in fact, the title only means that he is a moral leader who provides all believers with guidance. NSIC, on the other hand, is an established organization, which coordinates activities involving one or more of its foreign chapters, provides financial assistance to needy chapters, and most importantly, provides religious guidance.[4] It sponsors tours by Ikeda, prints a magazine that gives news from the various chapters, and publishes a variety of books on Nichiren Shoshu beliefs in several languages. Recent publications include a volume of the major writings of Nichiren and a dictionary of Buddhist terminology.

### The Soka Gakkai in the United States

The international movement got its start in the United States in 1960, when an organization known as Nichiren Shoshu Soka Gakkai (NSA) of America was established by a young Japanese emigrant, That Sadanaga, who later changed his name to George M. Williams.[5] Today, NSA, which is headquartered in Santa Monica, California, is highly organized. The present NSA organization starts at the smallest unit, a junior group, and proceeds upward to group, district, chapter, headquarters, territory, and joint-territory groups before reaching the NSA headquarters. There are several Nichiren Shoshu temples in America located in such places as Los Angeles and Honolulu. The movement operates the World Tribune Press, and publishes the World Tribune, a weekly eight-page newspaper, and a magazine, the Seikyo Times.

Soka Gakkai activities in the United States began much earlier than 1960. The first American-based members were believers of Japanese origin who settled in the United States in the late 1940s and 1950s and other resident Japanese who were converted in the U.S. The vast majority were Japanese women who married American servicemen in Japan and accompanied their husbands back to the United States. Other members were Japanese businessmen or government employees temporarily residing in the U.S. and Japanese students studying at American schools.[6] Numbers of believers, however, were very small. For example, during the late 1950s there were as few as thirty members in Hawaii, which today is a major center of membership.[7] The rate of growth in membership rose slowly in the 1960s, expanded rapidly in the early and mid-1970's and is tapering off in the 1980s, although growth continues.

The racial composition has changed dramatically over the years. In 1960 ninety-six percent of the membership was of Japanese extraction; only three percent were American whites. Changes since then have occurred as follows:

| Year | US White | US Black | Japanese Origin | Other |
|---|---|---|---|---|
| (Figures are percentages of total membership.) | | | | |
| 1960 | 3 | 1 | 96 | --- |
| 1965 | 14 | 5 | 77 | 4 |
| 1970 | 41 | 12 | 30 | 17 |
| 1972 | 63 | 22 | 11 | 4 |
| 1979 | 53 | 18 | 20 | 8 |
| 1981 | 55 | 19 | 14 | 9 |

Source: Inoue Nobutaka, Umi o Watatta Nihon Shukyo (Tokyo, 1985, p. 193.)

It is far easier to discuss the composition of the membership than to analyze why Nichiren Shoshu has done so well. Proselytization in the 1960s was done mainly on the street.[8] Members would approach people on the street, in restaurants, and elsewhere. One colleague reports that while he was waiting in line to enter a movie in Washington, D.C., a well-dressed young woman approached him and asked if he wanted to know the source of true happiness. After a brief conversation, she invited him to attend an NSA seminar, which he politely declined. In the early 1970s, NSA members held Buddhist "seminars" at about one hundred American campuses, where the basic teachings of Nichiren Shoshu were explained and the benefits of membership-- real happiness and material gain--were proclaimed.[9] Today most recruiting takes place with members inviting friends, colleagues, or acquaintances to district or smaller level meetings (zadankai).

Who joins and why? NSA Members have told me that they joined the movement because membership has given them some direction in life. They were dissatisfied with life and felt alone and estranged from the mainstream of society. NSA has given them something to believe in--a new set of goals and priorities. In addition, membership has put them into contact with other people with similar backgrounds and/or experiences. They often find consolation in being able to discuss their lives with sympathetic fellow members. Thus, the weekly or monthly meetings at people's homes can be as therapeutic as attendance at meetings of such groups as Alcoholics Anonymous.

The type of person who joins varies according to location. An official at the Washington meeting house stated that area members were generally young and tended to come from more affluent families.

> They were brought up as Christians, but had no real ties or affection for the Church. Because of the affluence of their parents, they did not have to work very hard at school or to worry about their futures. They are well educated, but tend to drift through life with no real commitment. Many experimented with drugs. They were looking for some commitment and direction in life and have found both in our movement. They are now free of drugs--we have

removed the drug culture from their lives and they are grateful to us because of this. [10]

He reported 8,000 members in the Washington area.

Guy McCloskey, Executive Director of the Washington office in 1986, reported a constituency near the headquarters building in Washington that was largely Black and not terrible affluent. He stated that the local membership closely reflected the character of the city's population as a whole and that NSA membership across the United States represents a cross-section of the American population. [11]

The director of the Boston chapter, however, stated in 1977 that membership in his area often came from younger lower-middle class Jews frustrated with their way of life.

Inoue Nobutaka, a young scholar at Kokugakuin University in Tokyo, reports in his book Umi o Watatta Nihon Shukyo that interest in the NSA grew in the late 1960s and early 1970s in such areas as California among younger people drifting through life without any real direction. At that time in California, there was a great general interest in Third World religions, so when these younger people were approached by an NSA member and invited to attend a meeting or seminar on Buddhism, many accepted. I myself remember such an invitation. As a student at Columbia University, I was riding to class one day when a handsome young woman approached me in the subway and asked if I was happy and satisfied with my religion. When I gave a noncommittal answer, she handed me a brochure inviting me to a Buddhist seminar. The brochure told how one could find real happiness through Nam-Myoho-Renge-Kyo, an invocation of the title of the Lotus Sutra.

Inoue gives the example of a young American who eventually joined NSA. This American went to church and Sunday school with his parents but stopped attending church around the age of fifteen. After graduating from a technical school, he became a hippie and moved to San Francisco around 1965, when that city became a haven for hippies from all over the country. To support himself, he became a taxi driver, but he had no particular ambitions or direction in life. He toyed around with some of the Third World religions of Indian origin that were in vogue then in California but found little that interested him or made him any happier. It wasn't until he was invited by one of his taxi customers to a buddhist meeting that he found something that was interesting and worth joining. With faith in this form of Buddhism, he claims that his negative attitude toward people changed, he developed a commitment to work,and he now has a clear sense of where he is going.12

One of the most prominent members of NSA is rock star Tina Turner. She and Patrick Duffy, star of the television soap opera Dallas, are longstanding members of NSA. In the 1960s Tina Turner and her former husband sang under the label "Ike and Tina Turner." Their songs were often played, but they never made it to the top of their profession. In the 1980s, however, Tina Turner has become one of the top rock stars in the world. In a 1986 interview with the Seikyo Shimbun, Turner explained why she joined NSA and what benefits she had gotten from her practice. She stated:

> I joined NSA 10 years ago. The first time I ever chanted daimoku was four years before my divorce. At that time, my father and the rest of my relatives were all Baptists. I didn't understand anything about Buddhism, so I used to chant daimoku and say, "Amen." But once I began chanting, good things kept happening to me. For instance, I had been experiencing some big trouble in my life, so I went

from chanting five times in a row to five minutes. Then I began to do gongyo...

My husband was against my practice, and it was hard for members to get close to me. But I continued to practice my faith, although I was by myself. As a result, I began to develop the strength to change what I knew I had to change. For example, I gained the determination to seek a divorce from my husband, whom I know I should have left years before. I was able to face and conquer many risks which arose from divorce (it was a most difficult period). Throughout the ordeal I continued to chant four hours a day. Then I was naturally able to keep my composure. No matter how unreasonable my husband became, internally I was able to stay a level above him. Although life with him had become very difficult, I was able to feel as if it was a kind of game because I was getting much stronger. Eventually it seemed as if a different sort of human being was emerging from within and I became convinced that I had changed a great deal.[13]

Her experience is unique because of her celebrity, but one meets with the same kinds of comments from the testimonials of more average members.

Despite its size and public activities, NSA receives much less publicity than other non-Western religious groups in the United States. NSA tries to blend itself in with the neighborhood, and its meeting halls are inconspicuous. For example, the Boston area chapter center is housed in an old Congregational Church in Quincy, and the Washington center looks like an ordinary brick office building in a lower middle class area on the Maryland border. In 1977 the Massachusetts director said that this policy was deliberate: "We want to become part of and accepted by the community. We seek no publicity and even discourage it. We can see what happens to other non-western religions when they get too much public attention. We watch all of the mistakes that the Moonies make and learn from their experiences."

NSA has flourished in the United States because it has indeed avoided the problems experienced by other Third World religious movements and cults that have attempted to attract American members. These other groups have failed largely because they became too controversial. The United States is still very much of a Christian country, and many Americans are suspicious of religions that are not Christian. Some of these groups like the "Moonies" (Unification Church) have become active politically, have spent vast sums of money to influence the political process in their favor, and have sought refuge from the tax laws while employing many people in various businesses. One recent case was that of an Indian whose religious cult took over a town in Oregon to the great annoyance of local residents.

Another fault of other Third World religious groups is their cult-like activities. They draw members away from society and seek to involve them in the group's activities on a full-time basis. The attempts of many parents and friends to "rescue" and "deprogram" loved ones from these cults often make the news and seem to win public support and sympathy. It seems that these cults make an active attempt to separate themselves from American society and from their American neighbors.

NSA has none of these faults. It goes out of its way to identify itself with such particular American themes as patriotism. For example, taking note of the fact that the United States was going to celebrate the hundredth anniversary of the Statue of Liberty with massive celebrations in New York City over the Independence Day weekend in 1986, NSA held its annual convention in New York City to coincide with the celebrations. The convention started on July 3rd at Madison Square Garden with a

"Youth Music Festival." Seven thousand young members from across the United States participated in brass bands and fife-and-drum corps, as well as in other artistic and gymnastic groups giving performances. Twenty thousand members congregated at the Garden for the convention.[14]

Earlier, NSA had done its best to arouse the patriotic fervor of its members and observers during the 1976 bicentennial celebrations in the United States. Parades, conferences, and demonstrations were held by the NSA throughout the United States. The major theme was the great advance of democracy in America over the last two hundred years.[15] An interesting essay, "NSA, Rekindling the American Spirit," by an NSA journalist, Gary Curtis, describes in a fascinating manner how the NSA has combined its own doctrines with its interpretation of American history in an effort to lay the groundwork for a Buddhist revolution in the United States. The underlying theme is that the American Revolution was the forerunner of the Buddhist revolution that must follow. America's founding fathers, like Shakyamuni in India, created a new social system, which was effective for a while, but has now decayed. Since American society has entered a "mappo-type age," a Buddhist revolution is now necessary to lead the United States into an age of "true democracy." Curtis writes:

> For many generations America was an example to the rest of the world. It demonstrated the advantages of democracy and the vast potential of citizens who are free to seek their happiness unrestrained. Many of the achievements that this country has made are directly due to the humanistic underpinnings of the American Revolution. That same tradition, while it has not always provided sound guidelines in these changing times, makes America especially suited to develop as a humanistic forerunner of a global movement based on the philosophy of life.

Before going into an analysis of America's potential today, perhaps we can best judge the adaptability of this nation to Nichiren Daishonin's true Buddhism by looking at the ideas upon which the nation was founded. There is good reason for such a historical perspective. According to the Buddhist concept of Go-Ko, the five principles of religious propagation, a philosophy has relevance to a country according to the conditions of the land, its people, and the time.

A Nation ready for Buddhism: The first principle is the specific nature of the philosophy, kyo. In this case, there is a distinct advantage to true Buddhism, as it is well suited to transform a society which lacks a clear-cut definition of life, a society which is largely mechanized and dehumanized and which places the highest priority on the well-being of its individual citizens.

The next principle, Ki, is the capacity of the people. No society is more adept at assimilating new ideas and putting them into practical use than America. Moreover, the growing distrust of traditional faiths and a desire for a way of life with relevance to day-to-day existence among Americans leaves them yearning for a supreme faith.

The third condition, Ji--the time, is again a ripe condition in the United States. This is a time when accepted values and ways of life are under stern examination. Many are being discarded, and there is discontent with worn out dreams of attaining happiness merely through affluence.

Koku, land, is the fourth criterion. America is a vast pool of ideas and concepts and has a culture which is undergoing astonishing change. The openness of the people, the close network of communications, the worldwide influence of American trends makes it a suitable environment for the spirited, contemporary movement of NSA. The last of these terms, Kyoho-rufu-no-Sengo, simply means 'sequence of propagation.' In other words, a new philosophy or ideal is suitable only if more elementary ideals have paved the way for it.

> There is a striking similarity between the humanistic
> doctrine of the revolutionary leaders of the 13
> colonies and the basic tenets of true Buddhism. The
> basic assumption of this essay is that there is a
> natural progression of thought from the concepts
> embedded in the original American spirit to the ideal
> of Buddhist democracy. Moreover, the dynamic
> principles of the life philosophy are what so many
> people of this country have sought. This is
> evidenced by the astonishing growth of NSA in
> America.[16]

Curtis goes on to say that the fundamental doctrine of
America's founders was the need to bring happiness to each
individual. By establishing such individual rights as freedom of
speech and belief, a person could define his own version of
happiness and live by his own standards. This doctrine, of course,
is basic to the Soka Gakkai's own philospohy. The United States,
he notes, has been a great nation in the past, but he implies that
Americans are now becoming discontented with their system and
desire a change. One source of discontent is the desire for new
religious values, which would give life a new meaning. However,
the desire for a renovation of society extends far beyond the need
for a new religion. Curtis states:

> Americans are always willing to seek a better way.
> Amid the clamor for a better society through
> revolution, we can hear the voices of growing ranks
> who cry out for a true way of life. The groundwork
> for that life has been laid. It is now time for the final
> construction of a humanistic society based on the
> philosophy of life. America, which gave the world its
> first taste of modern democracy and government of
> the common people, is a fertile field in which to plant
> the seeds for man's ultimate flower of humanistic
> civilization.[17]

Curtis has a good deal in common with certain other writers
who have called for a revival of the principles of the American

Revolution. These writers charge that Americans have departed from the social ideals outlined two hundred years ago and call on us to study our past in order to discover what we have lost. But Curtis himself is not seeking a revival of these traditional ideals; instead, he advocates their replacement by a more "modern" democratic set of doctrines which he believes will better meet the needs of the people in the twentieth century.

The NSA has assimilated American ideals, yet it avoids any participation in politics and shuns publicity, thus avoiding a "bad press." Its members are not drawn away from society. Members are supposed to pray daily at home with their families and are obliged to attend meetings on a weekly or monthly basis. NSA encourages its followers to become more active in their neighborhoods, to become "shining examples" that will encourage other people to join.

The result of these policies has been very good for NSA. Very few Americans are aware of its existence, which means that most people do not have any negative preconceived notions about the movement. This is in direct contrast to the "Moonies" who are well known and who have projected a very negative image. Thus, this lack of a negative image, as well as ideas and programs that are appalling to some Americans, means that NSA will continue to exist and may even grow in years to come.

### Chapters Outside the United States

NSA is the largest Soka Gakkai related group outside of Japan, but there are also offices in Britain, France, and elsewhere in Europe. Small chapters have recently been formed in several African countries. For example, the first chapter in Kenya was started by Takashi Yamada, an instructor of air traffic controllers at

Nairobi International Airport. Yamada worked there for five years. According to a Soka Gakkai magazine, "The first discussion meetings were very small, but today the waves of Kosen Rufu have reached to the Indian Ocean port of Mombassa and the Ugandan border city of Kisumu."[18] The Soka Gakkai has even tried to proselytize the faith in India, where there are still only a few hundred members. Nevertheless, the testimonial from one of its leaders sounds very much like testimonials from members in Japan. A reporter for SGI wrote the following article about the experiences of Vijay Konwar, subeditor of a Times of India publication:

> Mr. Konwar had long aspired to have a true friend, someone completely free of egoism who could understand everything about him. He had to conclude, however, that in a world like this the expectation of finding such a person was unrealistic. He had been very lonesome from childhood, and became increasingly isolated. He began to feel as though he were stalemated in life.
>
> It was in 1980, when he was 21, that he first heard of the true Buddhism. One day he went to visit his sister at the office where she worked; there he met Naveena Reddi (now chief secretary of Bhurat Soka Gakkai). She told him about Nichiren Shoshu Buddhism, describing it as a rational means to change one's karma. She spoke with such freshness and vigor that he made up his mind to give it a try,and so undertake his own human revolution.
>
> His mother and two sisters have also embraced the Daishonin's teachings. Though practicing Buddhism, his sister was able to overcome a serious illness, and relations among members of his family have improved tremendously; moreover, by taking part in activities, he has met many people whom he can trust completely and with whom he has formed deep and meaningful relationships. 'The only way to show my appreciation to the Gohonzon is to do shakubuku,' he says. And so he does, as district

chief in New Delhi, together with his sister, who was appointed to the same position in another city. Since he began practicing, his chief goal has been to show abundant proof of his happiness at work. As a result, colleagues often ask, 'Why do you look so happy every day?' He replies by explaining his experience.

Mr. Konwar contends that it is because of a sense of loyalty to Hinduism, which has long been the dominant religion in India, that his countrymen find it difficult to accept other religious teachings, even though in their hearts they may feel that their own religion is not very useful in their lives. Vijay, who had been a devout Hindu, explains that Indian people are so proud of their religion that many believe that Buddhism is only a part of Hinduism.

'Loyalty and happiness have nothing to do with each other,' notes Mr. Konwar. 'Which is more important,' he asks, 'to be loyal to a set of teachings or to be happy? If there is a teaching which gives people happiness in the true sense of the word, why not be more practical?'[19]

## Conclusion

The Soka Gakkai chapters abroad bear a close resemblance to those in Japan. Members abroad join for the same reasons as do their counterparts in Japan. The key difference between the home church and its chapters abroad is the total lack of political activity on the part of foreign chapters. There is very little hostility towards the NSA in the United States, which is a strong indication of the fact that the Soka Gakkai would have a far better reputation in Japan if it were to drop its political activities.

# NOTES

[1] _____, Soka Gakkai (Tokyo, 1983), p. 102.

[2] The figure of 500,000 members was supplied by Guy McCloskey, Executive Director of the Washington and SE Regional office of the Nichiren Shoshu Soka Gakkai of America in an interview on December 17, 1986 in Washington. Inoue Nobutaka, a Japanese scholar who studied Nichiren Shoshu in America in the early and mid-1980s concedes that while there may be over 200,000 believers in the United States, the actual hard-core membership must number half that. See Inoue Nobutaka, Umi o Watatta Shukyo (Tokyo, 1985) p. 156.

[3] Ibid.

[4] Interview with Yamaguchi Hiromu, Soka Gakkai International Bureau, August, 1984.

[5] Newsweek, June 5, 1972, p. 68.

[6] Inoue, p. 154.

[7] Ibid., p. 155.

[8] Ibid., pp. 173-78.

[9] Ibid., pp. 178-83.

[10] Interview with Eugene Y. Hirahara, Administrative Assistant, NSA branch in Washington, DC, June 1984.

[11] Interview with Guy McCloskey in Washington, D.C., December, 1986.

[12] Inoue, pp. 172-73.

[13] Soka Gakkai News, April, 1986, pp. 2-3.

[14] SGI, July 1986, p. 10.

[15]NSA Supplement, _Japan Times_, August 14, 1976, pp. B1-B8.

[16]Gary Curtis, "NSA Rekindling the American Spirit," _Japan Times_, August 14th, 1976, pp. B5-B7.

[17]Curtis, pp. B-B7.

[18]_SGI_, July, 1986, p. 21.

[19]_SGI_, July, 1986, p. 14.

# CHAPTER 7

## SPREADING THE WORD: ORGANIZATION
## AND
## SECULAR ACTIVITIES OF THE SOKA GAKKAI

The Soka Gakkai needs a vibrant organization to spread its evangelical message. It has a strong organizational structure to manage its activities and to recruit new members, as well as a huge and very profitable publishing empire which spreads the organization's eschatological message.

### Organization

The Soka Gakkai has a wide range of agencies and affiliated organizations that play two vital roles: extending its influence and teachings into various sectors of society and bringing people from the outside into the Soka Gakkai orbit. The Soka Gakkai sees itself as more than just a religious organization. It regards religion in isolation as being useless; a person cannot lock himself in a room in front of a gohonzon forever. A person has to function in society, and an important goal is to help a person be happier, more adept, and stronger in the outside world. Thus, the Soka Gakkai feels a special need to reach out and influence many people in various walks of life.

Another noteworthy aspect of these Soka Gakkai groups is that they bring members together, thus strengthening the cohesiveness of the movement. Prayer can be very lonely and individualistic in its nature; it is critical, but unless members know each other better and develop a sense of mutual trust and dependency, there will be little to hold the movement together. Japan is above all a group-oriented society, and if people are not encouraged to work together in groups, they might be tempted not to stay with the organization. Furthermore, commitment to the success of a concert, book, or magazine on peace, or to helping develop the professional abilities of another member will heighten devotion to the movement as a whole.

Called "The Great Cultural Movement," the Gakkai boasts a wide range of activities in its Cultural Department (frequent "Cultural Festivals"), a daily newspaper (the Seikyo Shimbun), a music movement, its own school system,and several art museums and research institutes.

### Organizational Management

The Soka Gakkai has two parts in its official organization: the central administration and local divisions. The main administrative structure manages all aspects of the Soka Gakkai and is made up of a fairly large staff of full-time workers. There are also various departments and divisions and the whole local apparatus of Soka Gakkai, which is run by volunteers without pay. Thus the organization is not that much different from many church organizations in the West: Every denomination has a central administrative office with a paid staff and director, as well as a publications bureau and other offices and officers. The strength of any church, however, comes from the work of individual members. For example, the vestry members in an Episcopalian church work hard and have considerable power, but they work as volunteers without pay.

The Soka Gakkai is run by a president. Below the president are a number of administrative bodies arranged in vertical order-- central, regional, and local. Below the president is a general director and a large number of vice-presidents. Reporting to these officials is the Board of Executive Directors, which is charged with formulating policy and making crucial decisions. Below the Board is the Central Committee, which runs the day-to-day affairs of the Gakkai. In all there are thirteen regional headquarters, each with its own regional chief and Regional Administrative Council. Below each regional headquarters are prefectural headquarters that oversee a number of local bodies.[1]

The Soka Gakkai is also divided into various divisions, including a Men's Division, a Women's Division, a Young Men's Division, a Young Women's Division, a Student Division, and a Future Division. These are essentially peer groups that deal with intercommunication and mobilization of the membership. Meetings and activities of these divisions are meant to foster a sense of fellowship. Members of the Men's Division, for example, undertake a number of important activities, including propagation of the faith, visits to the homes of members, frequent study sessions where they seek to strengthen their faith and knowledge, and occasional prayer meetings.

Members of the Women's Division engage in such activities as attending lectures and seminars on Nichiren Shoshu Buddhism, participating in discussion and prayer meetings, and visiting the homes of members. At a general meeting I attended at Soka University in 1984, leaders of the Women's Division split up into groups to hear seminars on Rissho Ankoku Ron and other topics and then met in the huge assembly hall to hear inspirational talks from Gakkai leaders.

The Young Men's Division (YMD) plays an active role in organizing and holding discussion meetings, Buddhist seminars, study courses, and youth culture festivals. At one meeting of the YMD I attended at Taiseki-Ji in 1984, Youth Division leaders were lecturing younger members on the meaning of peace and the role Nichiren Shoshu can play in fostering world peace. All participants were reading books on peace by Ikeda. Associated with this summer course was a series of cultural events, including amateur sumo matches and a huge outdoor gathering where all course participants joined in singing songs and watching fireworks. All these activities were carefully coordinated to enhance a feeling of belonging to the Gakkai, an understanding of Gakkai teachings, and a sense of fellowship among members. One active YMD member stated that in his group, more experienced members help new believers learn how to perform shakubuku adequately, help them answer questions about faith, and, in a sense, act as a "big brother" for the less experienced. "It is here where we form tight bonds of friendship. We can communicate with each other on a much closer basis than at an open meeting with a real diversity of people."

The YMD is also a training ground for future leaders of the Gakkai, and its leader in 1984, Ota Akihiro, is a person to watch. He clearly has much the same mesmerizing hold over members of the YMD as Ikeda has over the whole organization. There is also a tradition in the Gakkai of bringing up leaders from the YMD. Ikeda was prominent in the YMD when he was tapped by Toda as his successor.

The female counterpart to the Young Men's Division is the Young Women's Division (YWD). According to one Soka Gakkai brochure, the YWD is where "Soka Gakkai women lay the foundations of their future happiness. Through serious studies of the writings of Nichiren Daishonin and participation in various activities, they develop values that will serve them well in their homes and in society at large."[2] Day-to-day activities consist mainly of doctrinal study in small groups and participation in discussion meetings, but one notable preoccupation in recent years has been a tremendous amount of work in Japan interviewing older Japanese about their experiences during World War II. This material has been printed in numerous volumes and provides the reader with some of the best insights available in any language of the real horrors of the war. One YWD chapter in Fukuoka has been especially active, collecting material, putting together an excellent volume of its findings, and staging superb exhibits about the war in their local Gakkai headquarters.

The Student Division is for college students. Its most important activity is to set up chapters at schools where there are Gakkai members. Some of these chapters are very small while others can be huge. For example, at Waseda University, there is a small group of Soka Gakkai students which is dwarfed in size by the local Unification Church Chapter.[3] Regardless of size, these chapters provide member students with a sense of brotherhood and belonging. Some chapters form Buddhist study circles which organize lectures, seminars, and other cultural activities.

Another student group, the Future Division, is for junior high school and high school children, who meet once a month to study Nichiren Shoshu doctrines.

The Cultural Department of the Soka Gakkai consists of several smaller divisions divided by discipline: education, art, science, medicine, literature, academic, and international. One important function of these smaller divisions is to unite people with similar interests. A lawyer said that he belonged to the Lawyers' Division because it was the only chance he had to meet with other lawyers and discuss problems, concerns, and ideas that would only interest lawyers. A former professor says he goes to meetings of the Academic Division because "it is really refreshing to meet with other academics. I appreciate open meetings with people from a variety of backgrounds, but, boy, once in a while it is great to meet with other teachers and scholars, to hear about our

122

research and work, and to see how we as scholars can deepen our faith and scholarship concerning Nichiren Shoshu." Not long ago a group from the Medical Division went to China to compare notes with Chinese doctors. It was one of the first visits by Japanese doctors to China in a group since the reopening of China in the 1970s.

The Study Department is charged with the job of encouraging members to study and to interpret and write on the doctrines of Nichiren Shoshu. It gives exams on fixed occasions each year to test a member's understanding and knowledge of the sect's basic teachings and gives out "academic ranks" to those who pass the exams. Through these exams and by giving appropriate titles to successful candidates, the Gakkai gives a solid grounding to the faith of each member and rewards scholarship with impressive sounding titles.

## Publications

The Soka Gakkai runs its own publications empire. Publications serve two important purposes. First, they act as the major communications link between the organization and its members, spreading the teachings of the organization and of Nichiren Shoshu and giving news about Soka Gakkai activities. Second, they provide the Soka Gakkai with a major source of revenue. The Soka Gakkai does not demand any dues or contributions from members, but the average follower will spend a considerable sum of money each year subscribing to the Seikyo Shimbun, Daibyaku Rengei, and other regular publications, as well as the purchase of a variety of books by Ikeda and other Nichiren Shoshu and Soka Gakkai officials.[4]

The Seikyo Shimbun is the heart of the publications empire. It is the official newspaper of the Soka Gakkai. It was founded on

20 April 1951 through the efforts of Toda Josei. It started in the early 1950s as a twice-monthly two-page broadside with a small circulation, had a circulation of 3.5 million in the late 1960s and today is a daily with a circulation of nearly five million. According to Matsuoka Osamu, Executive Director and General Managing Editor of the Seikyo Press:

> Since its inception, the purpose of the newspaper has been the propagation of our Buddhism, to teach readers the basics of Nichiren's teachings. We report news on the flow of the <u>Kosen Rufu</u> movement, espouse the correct philosophy of Buddhism, and report on the experiences of members. We provide guidance lessons to strengthen the faith of members and to help them learn the correct practice of Buddhism. The news presented in the newspaper reflects the spirit of Buddhism.... People can get the spirit of Nichirne's teaching in contemporary society. We also promote the Soka Gakkai's programs for peace and justice.[5]

The first nine pages contain nothing but Soka Gakkai news. There are news articles about Soka Gakkai activities, features on various Gakkai programs, reports from various divisions and on important events, daily readings from and commentaries on the <u>Gosho</u>, and essays by invited guests on a variety of topics. For example, when Dr. Margaret Mead died in 1978, I was asked to write a commentary on her life; and in 1984, I wrote on my views of the Gakkai's peace efforts. In addition, there was a very brief page one article about my 1984 meeting with President Ikeda.

The last three pages deal with such secular topics as world and domestic news, sports news, and television listings. The <u>Seikyo Shimbun</u> receives world news from AP, UPI, AFB, and Tass. In addition, it has reporters stationed in seven world capitals. Its main offices are in Tokyo, near the Soka Gakkai headquarters, and there is a second office in western Japan, along

124

with nine branch offices and fifty-one smaller branch offices. Its facsimile network, according to Matsuoka, which ties the main office in all major cities, is the largest in Japan. According to Matsuoka:

> Most people read the Seikyo Shimbun for religious purposes and read other newspapers for hard news, but people who don't read very much can get a broad view of domestic and world news in compact form.[6]

President Ikeda is almost always followed by Seikyo Shimbun reporters, who seem to report on his every move. When he went to China in 1984, his trip was covered by two reporters and two photographers. When Ikeda met with top Chinese leaders, his activities were largely ignored by the secular Japanese press, although many reporters from other papers covered the trip and attended an Ikeda news conference. The Seikyo Shimbun, however, gave headline and in-depth coverage to every facet of the China trip.

The Seikyo Shimbun must be a profitable venture. It has a guaranteed sale of nearly five million newspapers a day and contains a great deal of advertising from a wide range of Japanese companies eager to sell their products to Soka Gakkai members. Mr. Matsuoka states that "all profits are used for religious purposes."[7]

The Seiko Shimbun Publishing Company, which is an official wing of the Soka Gakkai, also publishes a wide variety of other publications. There is, for example, the Daibyakurenge, a monthly theoretical and doctrinal journal with sales of 2.8 million. The magazine has excerpts from the Gosho, inspirational lectures on teachings of Nichiren Shoshu, fictionalized historical excerpts from scripture, and various reader interest stories. Whenever a member attends a azdankai, he is referred to that month's Gosho and is given a lecture on its implications for contemporary society. Study of the Gosho is also required reading for the Gakkai's Study Department examinations. Another popular publication is the Seikyo Graphic, a splashy weekly picture magazine with sales of eighty thousand. There are various divisional publications and two English publications, The Soka Gakkai News, a monthly newsletter, and SGI Graphic, a monthly color photo magazine. There are also numerous books by President Ikeda and other Soka Gakkai officials which can be bought at any large bookstore. Especially prominent is President Ikeda's fictionalized history of the Soka Gakkai, a multi-volume series of books, called Ningen Kakumei (Human Revolution) which hase sold millions of copies. Of equal importance are the published writings of Nichiren and various Nichiren Shoshu figures, as well as dictionaries and other resource books that help the reader understand these older documents.

Another area of publication has been Ikeda's "dialogues" with various scholars and other noted personalities around the world. The first dialogue was done in the early 1960s based on a series of conversations with the late British historian, Arnold Toynbee. Other personalities interviewed include the late French author, Andre Malraux.

The Soka Gakkai has also created a number of affiliated publishing companies that publish weekly or monthly articles intended primarily for nonmembers. These include Daisanbunmei and Ushio. Daisanbunmei carries a wide variety of shorter articles on world topics. For example, the October, 1984 issue carried stories on impressions of the drought in Africa, a view of the land of aborigines, and an essay on the value of the Soka Gakkai's peace movement. Ushio is today considered a widely acceptable intellectual magazine of the type popular with many educated

Japanese. It began in 1960 as an eighteen page theoretical magazine on politics published for Gakkai members. It also carried articles by Soka Gakkai leaders. After January 1963, however, the Soka Gakkai transformed Ushio from a sectarian magazine into a typical Japanese intellectual magazine. An examination of any issue will give no hint that it is still a Soka Gakkai publication. It is published by the Ushio Shuppan Sha, an independent affiliate of the Soka Gakkai. There are few, if any, articles by Gakkai leaders. Japanese intellectuals, who were at first a bit reluctant to contribute, now write regularly for the magazine, and I know a good number of Japanese scholars not affiliated with the Soka Gakkai who read it on occasion.

### Education

Education has always played a very special role in the Soka Gakkai's history and thinking. In the 1930s the Gakkai's "founding father," Makiguchi Tsunesaburo, was greatly interested in educational reform, as well as religion. Toda Josei, the second president, was himself a teacher. According to a Soka Gakkai pamphlet:

> Toda inherited Makiguchi's ideas and did much to give them form. It was, however, under the leadership of Third President Daisaku Ikeda that the Soka Gakkai was able to put that educational philosophy into practice. Since world peace and cultural development ultimately depend upon the actions of human beings, the way to build a foundation for peace and culture in the world is to nurture people rich in humanity and culture. Through the creation of Soka Gakuen and Soka University, the Soka Gakkai is contributing directly to the enrichment of society.[8]

The Soka Gakkai's educational system is actually quite small: It consists of a kindergarten in Sapporo, elementary schools in Tokyo and Osaka, coeducational junior and senior high schools near Tokyo and Osaka, Soka University, located on the outskirts of Hachoji about thirty miles from downtown Tokyo, and Soka women's (junior) College located at Hachoji.

More recently the Soka Gakkai has opened a junior college for women on the Soka University campus, has established a European Center in Paris, and is working on an American campus near San Diego, California. According to plans for the American campus, the American Language Center will offer Japanese students courses in the English Language, along with American studies courses that include American History, politics, economics, and culture. The second phase calls for offering courses in the Japanese language to Americans and non-American residents in the United States. Classes there are expected to begin in 1987.[9]

The Soka Gakkai is not very clear as to what it means by "humanistic education." It claims that it must follow national law and give students a very traditional nonsectarian education. Its leaders insist that the schools are open to both members and nonmembers. When I asked Yamazaki Hisami, a senior vice-president of the Soka Gakkai and head of the Board of Trustees at Soka University to explain what is meant by "humanistic education," he replied:

> It does not mean the direct teaching of Soka Gakkai and Nichiren Shoshu doctrines in the classroom. That goes against the spirit of the law that governs education in this country and would be difficult to implement because at Soka University, at least twenty percent of the student body are not Soka Gakkai members and about half of the teachers in our school system do not belong. But what we do offer our students is close personal attention.
>
> One of the problems with Japanese education is the large size of classes, lack of personal relationships

between teacher and student, and an emphasis on rote learning that does not allow the average student to think on his own feet. President Makiguchi believed that a student would prosper if he were treated with respect and was given some real attention. If you look at Soka University, for example, we have many small seminars, classes are not quite as big as at other schools, and there is much contact and great rapport between student and teacher. In a general sense we seek to nurture talent and develop each student to his greatest potential--by working directly with students we can accomplish far more for the student than can most other Japanese schools.[10]

It is difficult for an outsider to assess these comments and to comment on the overall quality of the Soka Gakkai educational system. To visit the facilities at Soka University and at Soka Women's Junior College is to marvel at the most modern technology, the very well-equipped and stocked libraries, and the newest and cleanest of buildings. The scholarship of faculty members is also good to excellent. I have read articles by some Soka University professors and have heard some present papers at international symposia. The quality of their work certainly ranks with the best. In an effort to develop a good faculty quickly, the university enticed many noted professors/scholars with promises of higher salaries, better working conditions, and enhanced opportunities for research. One noted Japanese scholar, not a member but very familiar with the school, noted: "I would not rank Soka University in the same league as Tokyo University and Keio University, but it has come a very long way since its inception in 1971, and is now one of the better colleges in Japan."

Despite Soka Gakkai denials, however, one can see that the school system can very well be a socializing agency with converting potential. One Soka University professor remarked once half-jokingly that "when they enter, a quarter of our students may not be Gakkai members, but by the time they graduate we will have got them and virtually all of our graduates will be members." There is at least some truth to this statement. The majority of students are members whose values and support for the organization are probably strengthened. Nonmember students find themselves in a distinct minority and will probably receive many direct and indirect pressures to join the movement.

## Other Activities

The Soka Gakkai offers members a wide variety of cultural activities. A major activity is in music. The Soka Gakkai's Fife and Drum Corps, with 20,000 members or more nationwide, performs at a variety of functions at home and abroad. Various choruses give concerts, as does the Min-On Concert Association. The Music Corps which consists of parade, wind instrument, light, and orchestra sections, performs at Gakkai cultural festivals, parades, and other events. The two Fuji art museums have limited, but interesting collections of art and artifacts. The Oriental Institute of Academic Research publishes books on Buddhism and offers a course of doctrinal studies on Nichiren Shoshu.[11]

## NOTES

[1]Soka Gakkai (Tokyo, 1983), p. 26.

[2]Ibid., p. 40.

[3]Interview with Shimada Yukio, Professor of International Law at Waseda, Summer, 1985.

[4]In the late 1960s Murata Kiyoaki, a journalist who won the trust of the Soka Gakkai, reported on Soka Gakkai finances as follows:

> Soka Gakkai is one of the most affluent associations in Japan, although its members do not pay dues as such. Its annual budget is said to be about 2,600,000,000 yen ($7,222,000), but real income is considerably higher. Of this amount, about 1,600,000,000 is contributed by the Finance Department, whose approximately 400,000 members are replaced annually. Each member of this department is required to pay 4,000 yen (slightly over $11) annually in four installments. A further one billion yen is believed to come from the sale of Soka Gakkai books and periodicals.

Source: Murata, Japan's New Buddhism (Tokyo, 1969), p. 144.

James White makes the important point that another important source of income in the past has been donation drives from members. Such drives are staged for special construction projects, but the response is usually so great that the costs of a project are usually surpassed.

[5]Interview with Matsuoka Osamu, Tokyo, June 12, 1984.

[6]Ibid.

[7]Interview.

[8]Soka Gakkai (Tokyo, 1983), p. 93.

[9]Soka Gakkai News (May, 1986), p. 11. The site for the American campus was relocated to Los Angeles. Los Angeles campus opened in February 1987.

[10]Interview with Yamazaki Hisami, Soka Gakkai Senior Vice President, in Tokyo, 1 August 1984.

[11]Ibid., Murata Kiyoaki

# CHAPTER 8

## THE SOKA GAKKAI AND POLITICS

The Soka Gakkai insists that if one is to change the world, political action is necessary. Gakkai leaders fully realize that politics is what moves society and that the Soka Gakkai must have some political role to realize its own dreams. During the 1950s and 1960s, the Soka Gakkai was directly involved in electoral politics, but in the 1970s and 1980s, direct action has been replaced by indirect pressure. Soka Gakkai members continue to support the Gakkai's former party, the Komeito, and the Gakkai is involved in a variety of pressure efforts, including its peace movement, which are designed to bring public opinion to its side on a variety of issues.

The Soka Gakkai's eschatological message is that the world is doomed unless we rid ourselves of the menace of nuclear weapons. A deeper message, however, is that the world will never know peace until the world is led by men who truly want peace. The implication is that only people exposed to the "true Buddhism" of Nichiren will understand the true meaning of peace. In any case, the Soka Gakkai has justified its domestic and international involvement by saying that politics will be improved when people who know Buddhism are involved.

The intense and extremely successful involvement of the Soka Gakkai in domestic politics is a phenomenon without parallel among contemporary Japanese religious organizations. The Komeito, a political party that the Gakkai created in the mid-1960s, has won many parliamentary seats. In the 1970s and 1980s, the

Komeito has generally been the third ranking party in the Diet, putting many Soka Gakkai members into positions of public power and trust.

The Soka Gakkai's actual participation in electoral politics began in April 1955, when it ran 54 candidates in a series of local elections as independents and lost only one race. One must not forget that one of the traditions of modern Japanese politics is to run candidates only when you have supporters and a reasonable chance of winning the election. The Gakkai elected nine candidates to the House of Councilors in the 1956 and 1958 elections and was successful in fifteen races in 1962. Encouraged by its own early successes, the Gakkai formed a political organization known as the Komei Seiji Remmei ("Clean Government League") in 1962 and transformed this loosely organized group into the Komeito in 1964, when it decided to enter candidates in the next general election for the Lower House of the Diet. It won twenty-five seats in the 1965 elections and forty-seven in 1969. Although in May of 1970 the Gakkai announced that it was severing its official ties with the Komeito, a strong emotional attachment and dual membership keep the two organizations close, at least in a general sense. In the 1986 national elections the Komeito retained its roughly ten percent share of the vote and seats in the Diet at a time when other opposition parties lost many votes to the victorious Liberal Democratic Party (LDP).

The Soka Gakkai insists that it detached itself from the Komeito because the Komeito had grown big enough to stand on its own. Close ties with the Gakkai were necessary as long as the party was small and weak--going through its "incubator" stage. One also gets the impression from Gakkai leaders that day-to-day involvement in their hectic world of Japanese politics distracted them from their primary interests in religion. As one Gakkai official notes, "We are a purely religious organization and our sole purpose is the promotion of the doctrines of Nichiren Shoshu."[1] Soka Gakkai leaders insist that the party's function today is to promote and defend matters of importance to the Gakkai, including defense of Japan's "peace constitution," social welfare, and the freedom of religion.[2]

Outside observers say that the Soka Gakkai publicly severed ties with the Komeito because of public criticism concerning the involvement of a purely religious group in party politics at a time when the separation of church and state has become an important issue in Japanese politics. There is also the feeling that the Komeito could not broaden its public appeal as long as it was so closely affiliated with the Gakkai and completely dependent on Gakkai support and votes. An "independent" party could attract votes from non-Gakkai voters. There were also one or two embarrassing scandals involving the Soka Gakkai and its involvement in politics around 1970, and separation from the political world was a graceful way for the Gakkai to move away from these scandals.

Since its formal split from the Komeito in May 1970, the Soka Gakkai has maintained that it is a religious organization with no direct involvement in or commitment to politics. Statements on specific aspects of Japanese politics are now rare by Gakkai leaders, and there is a slow but steadily growing separation between the two organizations at least in the daily conduct of their affairs. Yano Junya, the chairman of the Komeito, explains the relationship best:

> By 1970 we had grown strong enough to be on our own. As is the case with Ushio (magazine), which the Soka Gakkai started as one of its own journals and which now runs itself, the Gakkai nurtured us and then let us go. Frankly, it was cumbersome to

have a religious organization run the daily affairs of a major political party.

Today we are totally separate, but strong links of friendship remain. In my religious and private life, I am an eager and enthusiastic member of the Soka Gakkai and I hope I reflect some of its humanitarian principles in the conduct of politics, but when you are wheeling-and-dealing in the topsy-turvy world of Japanese politics, the Komeito must take its own initiative and work day-to-day as an independent body. The same applies to policy formation. The Soka Gakkai does not get involved in the making of defense policy and we don't try to counter their influence in making religious decisions.[3]

There are, however, still some important connections between the Soka Gakkai and the Komeito. There is, for example, the very strong emotional bond between the two organizations. The Soka Gakkai created the Komeito and gave it some direction. A vast majority of the Komeito Dietmen have been Soka Gakkai members. In the past few elections only, a very small handful of non-Soka Gakkai members have run under the Komeito banner and have won. It is as if the Komeito will run a few token non-Soka Gakkai members now and then to give the guise of more independence. Finally, there is the fact that a vast majority of Komeito votes in elections come from Soka Gakkai members. The public still associates the Soka Gakkai with the Komeito. A 1984 survey of 100 Waseda students in 1984 found that all of the 100 students interviewed connected the Soka Gakkai with the Komeito and said that they would not vote for the party because of their aversion for its religious founder.[4]

There is also the question of the political role of Ikeda Daisaku in the 1980s. His stated role is that of a spiritual leader training younger people for future leadership of the Gakkai.[5] Nonetheless, Komeito leaders will consult him on occasion concerning policy decisions and after Ikeda's trips to China will occasionally talk with him to learn more about his meetings with Chinese leaders.[6] Some journalists who cover Diet proceedings state that Ikeda is still a force in Japanese politics working behind the scenes to wheel-and-deal. According to one journalist:

> Ikeda still wants political power, but not open involvement. He likes to work indirectly behind the scenes and wants to become an unseen power-broker like one of the cloistered retired shoguns of the past.[7]

However, I have never found any direct evidence linking Ikeda with active political life today.

### The Political Philosophy of the Soka Gakkai

The Soka Gakkai's theories about the relationship of government and the people are presented in Ikeda's book, Seiji to Shukyo (Politics and Religion), first published in 1965. Ikeda prepared this work almost simultaneously with the formation of the Komeito in 1964, and he most likely wrote it as a justification for his organization's entry into party politics. The first half of this study contains an abbreviated history of Western and Japanese political theory and discusses the role of politics and society. Later chapters reveal the political goals of the Soka Gakkai.

The Soka Gakkai's conventional view of national politics resembles its view of international relations. The Gakkai does not propose to alter institutions of government, but it does call for the fusion of political ideas with a religious spirit of benevolence derived from Buddhism. This fusion can provide government with a firm philosophical base, inspire politicians to work for the welfare of the people, and educate the public to play a more active role in government and politics. The Soka Gakkai further contends that

138

national and social problems will abate when the spiritual unity of the nation is attained.

The Soka Gakkai's view of the nation-state is very close to that of many contemporary political scientists. The state, notes Ikeda, contains three important elements--people, territory, and sovereignty--and can be defined as a "local community of persons with a general and supreme organization of government."[8] The national government is seen as a dominant, controlling and active force in a nation, existing to promote social and political objectives through the use of law and power.[9] This view of government as the dominant institution of society makes it inevitable for the Gakkai to take politics into consideration in formulating plans for the reformation of society.

Ikeda emphasizes that political parties play an important part in politics in modern states because they act as an essential link between government and the people. Individual politicians working on their own have little chance of achieving their major goals unless they are able to form a working relationship with a respectable number of like-minded men and can win the support of a significant proportion of the population; then they stand at least some chance for success. Successful political parties must have a broad base of support and must concern themselves with a wide range of issues.[10] Only then can a political system really represent the people.

The Gakkai defines politics as a technique to organize and unify the diverse forces and functions of society and to control the conduct of individuals through public power. Consequently, politics is not an end in itself, but a means of social control that is applied by the state and society to guide a nation's economy and all other diverse aspects of society that government is forced to regulate.[11] Needless to say, society could not function without some form of political structure.

Soka Gakkai officials feel that the two essential elements of politics are man and law. Men employ power in government to benefit or victimize the public, and there is no way an active member of society can escape its effect. The use of power, however, requires rules that regulate both the way authority can be used and the actions of those who wield it. Even the most dictatorial or arbitrary forms of government cannot survive without basic regulations to guide this conduct from one day to the next. Interpreted in a far broader sense, however, law is based on philosophy, which is still another important ingredient in political systems. Government must be based on a broad and embracing philosophy which inspires all citizens to regulate their lives and behavior in a manner appropriate to their society as a whole.[12]

### The Soka Gakkai and Political Idealism

Ikeda feels that there are basically two kinds of political systems: one type benefits society as a whole; the other serves the interests of a limited few at the expense of everyone else. Mankind, through its long history, has developed forms of government that serve only limited minority interests; that is, the vast majority of people have been forced to suffer because their leaders have so rarely acted on their behalf.[13] Generally they have been asked to make sacrifices for their leaders, who in turn have exploited them.[14]

Ikeda, however, contends that politics should not lead to suffering. Indeed, by working for everybody, government can play an important role in the creation of a happy, peaceful and prosperous society. Thus, politics should not be directed toward protecting the prosperity of any one class but should give all people an equal chance to enjoy happiness by providing them with the opportunity to realize their personal values. The ideal of politics must lie in the perfect coordination of the happiness of all individuals and the prosperity of society as a whole.[15]

Ikeda surveyed the political systems available to man and concluded that democracy comes closest to matching his ideal of politics:

> In general, the term "democracy" implies a thought or philosophic ideology, and democratic government means political or social systems. Democracy, as an idea, is centered around liberty, equality, and respect for humanity. Democratic government, basing itself on these principles, is, as Lincoln put it, "government of the people, by the people and for the people." In political theory, government for the people is an especially conspicuous feature of democratic government.[16]

But Ikeda asserts that Abraham Lincoln's eloquent words mean different things to different people. Various regimes around the world, including those in ruthless totalitarian states, have claimed that they are providing government "for the people." Democracy itself is a very loose term that has been defined in many ways. There is, for example, social democracy in Western Europe, "People's Democracy" in Eastern Europe and China, and liberal democracy in the United States.[17] Ikeda believes that it is his main task to determine the basic elements of "true" democracy.

Ikeda feels that the two fundamental rights for which men fought for centuries are equality and freedom, and he insists that no social and political system can be called democratic without them. It is an unfortunate fact of life, however, that in the contemporary world, equality and freedom are generally treated as contradictory concepts which cannot be incorporated in one society.[18] If one stresses absolute equality, for example, rigid standards must be developed to insure that no person will be discriminated against in any way. Such a system establishes a low common denominator that prevents the person with special talents or interests from reaching a position in life commensurate with his talents or inclinations. On the other hand, a system that stresses personal freedom and allows the individual to strive for his own values will exhibit various forms of inequality and differences in social standing. Ikeda emphasizes that mankind must establish a social system based on both equality and freedom that works toward an equilibrium between the two.[19]

The Soka Gakkai states that "true freedom" for all individuals is one of its most cherished goals and is the theme of its Human Revolution. Ikeda and other Gakkai theorists state that throughout history man has been fighting for freedom from something. Thus, man has battled for freedom from government suppression, from religious oppression, and from racial discrimination. To a large extent this struggle has been successful: Today people in Japan and the West are less intimidated by their governments than in the past; they can worship as they please and there is now less racial discrimination than there was only a few decades ago.[20]

The Soka Gakkai feels that despite these gains, few men are truly free. Their freedom is greatly restricted by such things as poverty, starvation, illness, and personal worry. At the same time, many people are so obsessed with greed, animosity, and hatred that they have virtually no ability, time, or strength to overcome their torments. Their problem is that they are dominated by evil karmas, which prevent them from obtaining any degree of permanent happiness. Only by overcoming their evil karmas by subscribing to the doctrines of Nichiren will they have a chance to obtain freedom in the true sense of the word.[21]

The Soka Gakkai insists that only its doctrines can bring "true equality." Many nations now guarantee their citizens equality before the law, but social inequality exists everywhere. Racial discrimination, for example, is an international phenomenon, which, along with other forms of discrimination, is practiced even in the Soviet Union, where society is supposed to be egalitarian. Ikeda asserts that true equality implies a spirit of mercy and compassion for all other beings, as well as respect for human dignity, and that such feelings may be nurtured only through the teachings of Nichiren and advancement to the higher realms of life.

The Soka Gakkai asserts that "true" freedom and equality cannot be established by government edict or social sanctions. Instead, they must "well up in the hearts of men." This idea goes back to the belief that as long as men are encumbered with bad karmas, society will be bad, and individuals will suffer many indignities in life. As long as the average man lacks a sense of propriety and compassion, his leaders cannot be expected to exhibit these virtues. Since even ruthless dictators must have at least some public support, any basic changes among the majority of the people of a state will force the rulers to alter their policies. Consequently, a nation that is guided by leaders who are inspired by Buddhist benevolence will be more likely to have a superior form of government. Since only the teachings of Nichiren Buddhism can help man to realize the blessings of freedom and equality, a "true democracy" can materialize only through the implementation of the Human Revolution in each nation.

## Obutsu Myogo and Politics

President Ikeda feels that the primary social role of religion is to remove the basic causes of human unhappiness and to teach people to gain true happiness, harmony, and prosperity in life.

Religion is essential for the philosophical, social, and political betterment of society as a whole, and it must enter into every aspect of social life, including politics, in order that change for the better may occur. Consequently, the Gakkai calls for a fundamental fusion of religious idealism and practical politics. Since politics is a necessary tool for the government of men, politicians need a practical philosophy to guide them, and religion --especially one that teaches man about the true aspects of life--is the only system of thought that can guide government leaders toward the betterment of society.[22]

Obutsu myogo, which literally translated means "the fusion of politics and religion," does not mean the imposition of a state religion. The Soka Gakkai denies having any desire to create a theocracy, even though it formed a political party. Instead, Gakkai leaders hope to bring politics and religion together by persuading the people that they must accept "true" Buddhism as the basis of everybody's way of life. When enough people have been converted--perhaps a majority of the population--they will elect responsible public officials who will purify government and will work to help, rather than hinder, true social progresses. The Soka Gakkai also calls for the election of a few responsible members of the Diet who have been imbued with the doctrines of Nichiren Shoshu and who will serve as both "watchdogs" and "gadflies" to help protect the Japanese people from the evils of selfish politicians. These members of the Diet would act as the "conscience" of the assembly, even though they were few in number.[23]

### Obutsu Myogo: Human Socialism and Buddhist Democracy

The Soka Gakkai has introduced two concepts, Human Socialism (Ningen Shakaishugi) and Buddhist Democracy (Buppo

Minshushugi), which together represent the ideals of the practical politics and religious principles (Obutsu Myogo), the philosophy society must adopt for the creation of a truly democratic society.

Human Socialism is the Soka Gakkai's program for the economic reconstruction of society. Gakkai leaders feel that the two dominant economic systems of the world today, capitalism and socialism (or Marxism), contain both positive and negative aspects, and they hope to bring together that which is good in both systems and eliminate that which is bad. The democratic ideals of Nichiren Shoshu, of course, would provide this new system with a fundamental philosophy. Ikeda feels that an ideal economic system must incorporate the three values of Makiguchi Tsunesaburo: "Human life is the pursuit of value; when man acquires the values of beauty, gain and good, he will become happy. The ideal society is one in which all people can acquire all of these values."[24] Each person must be allowed to attain his own measure of beauty and gain in his own life, and there must be an emphasis on the improvement of society as a whole.[25]

Ikeda praises capitalism because it permits people to seek beauty and gain for themselves, but he faults it because it lacks incentives for people to seek the good and to make "contributions to society."[26] In a capitalistic society, the individual through his own initiative may choose any field of endeavor to seek beauty and gain, but since there is far more emphasis on the individual than on society as a whole, inevitably there are people who are impoverished by capitalism's "excessively bitter competition."[27] Ikeda says that capitalism denies man an opportunity to strive for "true freedom" and "true equality" because so many people are denied the chance to attain any of these values--beauty, gain, and good. To realize "true democracy" a society must also incorporate good.[28] Too often capitalists concentrate on their own needs and institute few, if any, programs intended to benefit the underprivileged and to bring about a more egalitarian society.

Socialism, on the other hand, is praised for its emphasis on social good but is criticized for its lack of concern for beauty and gain.[29] According to the Soka Gakkai, socialists stress a structural reformation of society with an emphasis on equality. Special attention is devoted to public programs that insure that all people will have access to the basic necessities of life, but, unfortunately, socialists tend to view life in terms of society as a whole rather than as a group of distinct individuals. Instead, people must accept the dictates of the state and must follow the rigid guidelines laid down by government, even if it means sacrificing their individual needs.[30]

The Soka Gakkai recognizes the need for the state to provide people with comprehensive programs to alleviate the kinds of problems that develop in a capitalistic society. However, it believes that people cannot be happy under a system of government that stifles individual freedom and initiative.[31] Socialism was founded to overcome economic inequality, but, according to Ikeda, socialists do not seem to realize that human society is composed of individuals, each of whom has his own distinct characteristics and goals. Even if material equality could be attained, there would still be undeniable differences in the value an individual attached to material items equally distributed to all. Consequently, traditional socialism is an unacceptable doctrine.

The Soka Gakkai's practical solution to the imbalances of socialism and capitalism is the creation of a democratic welfare state in which a humane and unselfish government would provide all people with good and inexpensive health care, a superior and less rigid education, and a pollution-free environment. There would be an effort to improve vastly the physical condition of cities:

Roads would be improved, slums would be torn down and replaced with good public housing, and strict anti-pollution codes would be enforced with vigor. Government would help the needy with improved social services and adequate welfare programs.[32]

The state, however, would not be overbearing. There would be a free and open social and economic environment that permitted people to live as they chose.[33] A person who desired a college education and a good job would be given every chance to study and to work; his success would depend upon his ability, his determination, and the availability of jobs. Government would ensure that such things as utter poverty, curable sicknesses, and unfair legal and social laws would not stand in his way. It would be up to the individual, however, to create his own value.[34]

The Gakkai asserts that capitalism and socialism should be combined with a human touch to create Human Socialism. The government should be an agency to restructure society, so that each person can have an equal chance to establish both personal and social values to the maximum degree. This Human Socialism is socialism imbued with a view of man as an individual: "Humanitarian Socialism creates a situation where every person can establish his own self and arrive at his potential ability." There should be an emphasis on "mutual aid" so that each person can contribute to the good of others while improving himself.[35]

Religion, of course, plays a major role in the creation of this new system. The Buddhism of Nichiren Shoshu is believed to have the power to teach people appropriate values, which they will employ for their own and the general welfare of mankind. Honest and compassionate capitalists will still seek to improve their own way of life but at the same time will contribute to the good of society. Individuals will prosper because there will be no barriers in the way of attaining personal values, and society will prosper because the emphasis on social good will lead to the disappearance of unfair economic practices and class conflict. The realization of the Human Revolution and <u>kosen rufu</u> are prerequisites for such a development since, without this development, man will still reside in the lower realms of life.

The economic and social ideals of Human Socialism read well on paper, but can they be brought to fruition? One problem is money. It would cost vast sums to implement even a few of the Gakkai's programs, and these funds would eventually have to come from the wallets of all wage earners. Vastly higher taxes, in turn, would make life harder and certainly less free. This is a contradiction that the Gakkai must solve before it can make realistic plans. As yet social democracy in Great Britain and Sweden has many flaws that must be worked out if people's real needs are to be met. For example, government may borrow vast sums of money for large projects today, but eventually everybody in society must pay the bill.

## Formation of the Buddhist State

Buddhist democracy, the political philosophy that the Soka Gakkai espouses for the creation of its welfare state, is intended to provide politics with a firm philosophy that will guide Japan's government toward the creation of a free and just society based on true equality.[36] Buddhist democracy is said to be a superior doctrine because it is based on the teachings of Nichiren Shoshu, which provide relief from evil karma. All men are inherently equal because, according to the theory of Ten Worlds, the potential for Buddhahood is within them. Buddhist democracy through Nichiren Shoshu offers all people the same opportunity to rid themselves of suffering and misery and to attain true happiness.[37] The Soka Gakkai maintains that it is the only form of democracy that exists for the benefit of all people without distinctions of race, creed, or social origin, since it emphasizes a spiritual rebirth that can take place in any person who has faith in the doctrines of Nichiren Shoshu. No other doctrine can remove unhappiness from the lives of men and teach them to respect the dignity and equality of others.[38] By implication, if Japan's leaders, along with the public, were to adopt the "true" Buddhism, the leaders would have the ability and compassion to lead Japan toward a Buddhist paradise.

Buddhist democracy, in other words, carries the philosophy of Nichiren Shoshu into the world of politics. It calls for the formation of a Buddhist state with a civil government that bases its policies on the teachings of society's modern Sangha, the Gakkai, and Nichiren Shoshu. Ikeda's major hero in history is King Ashoka of India, who is said to have created a tolerant Buddhist government in India more than 2,000 years ago.[39] His comments about Ashoka indicate that Ikeda envisions a state run by an independent civil government that would sympathize with the ideals of the Sangha and would initiate legislation so that the Sangha would penetrate more deeply into society. The dominant force, of course, would be the Soka Gakkai because it espouses religious and social doctrines that permeate all aspects of life.

The Soka Gakkai asserts that its brief foray into politics represents a small part of its overall interest in the political realm. Its leaders feel that their primary task is to enlighten men, not to tamper with the actual political process. Because people today are totally ignorant of and confused about the actual laws of life itself, they accept a kind of political process which fosters inequality, corruption, and poor representation of popular aspirations. The Soka Gakkai hopes to educate men about the laws of life through the Human Revolution and kosen rufu so that they will become aware of the shoddiness of their present political process. An enlightened person, for example, will understand the meaning of true freedom and equality and will be able to spot the imperfections that exist today. He will espouse the concepts of Human Socialism and Buddhist Democracy and of his own accord--without the aid of the Soka Gakkai--will choose to work to improve the political process.

# NOTES

[1]Statement made by Yamaguchi Hiromu, an official in the Soka Gakkai's Inter Bureau, in Tokyo in August, 1985.

[2]Interview with Akiyama Tomiya, Director of the Soka Gakkai's International Bu Tokyo, July, 1984.

[3]Interview with Yano Juhya, Secretary-General of the Komeito, 31 July 1984 in Office Building, Tokyo. Yano became party chairman in 1987.

[4]Survey of 100 Waseda University Students conducted in July, 1984 by the author.

[5]Interview with Ikeda Daisaku on 14 July 1984 at Soka University near Tokyo.

[6]Yano Interview

[7]Interview with Tsukamoto Akira, political correspondent at the Diet for the Television Broadcasting System, July 1984.

[8]Ikeda Daisaku, Seiji to Shukyo (Tokyo, 1969), p. 91.

[9]Ibid.

[10]Ibid., pp. 113-16.

[11]Ibid., pp. 105-13.

[12]Ibid., pp. 93-94.

[13]Ibid., pp. 100-8.

[14]"Buppo to Ningen Kakumei," Daibyaku Renge, No. 302 (June, 1976), pp. 78-79.

[15]Ikeda, Seiji, pp. 101-5.

[16]Ibid., p. 143.

[17]Ibid., pp. 143-45.

[18]Ibid.

[19]Ibid., pp. 143-48.

[20]Conclusion of a Soka Gakkai Seminar on Politics, 31 August 1976 in Tokyo.

[21]Ibid.

[22]Ohara Teruhisa, Suematsu Yoshinori and Hirano Tomosaburo, Soka Gakkai no Seimei no Seiki no Funade (Tokyo, 1975), pp. 47-69.

[23]Ibid.

[24]Ikeda, Seiji, p. 219.

[25]Ibid., pp. 219-20.

[26]Ibid., pp. 220-22.

[27]Ibid.

[28]Ibid.

[29]Ibid.

[30]Ibid.

[31]Ibid., pp. 221-22.

[32]Ohara, et al., pp. 57-59.

[33]Ibid.

[34]Ibid.

[35]Ibid.

[36]Ikeda, Seiji, pp. 208-9.

[37]Ibid., pp. 210-17.

[38]Ibid.

[39]Ikeda Daisaku, Watashi no Bukkyokan (Tokyo, 1974), pp. 55-76.

# CHAPTER 9

## SOKA GAKKAI DIPLOMACY AND CHINA

The Soka Gakkai's involvement in international politics is much less documented than its history in the domestic political realm. Nevertheless, there are statements in virtually every Gakkai publication about the danger of Armageddon and articles about the efforts of Soka Gakkai "statesmen," such as Ikeda Daisaku, during their missions for peace. There is often a picture of Ikeda meeting with some head of state, ambassador, or important cultural figure. Soka Gakkai President Akiya states that the Japanese still have an "Island mentality," meaning that the world view of the average Japanese is far too parochial.

> Part of the purpose of the Soka Gakkai peace movement is to foster a broader world view so that Japanese can better understand foreigners. Closer contacts between Japanese and people elsewhere will lead to greater understanding and a subsequent reduction in tensions. When Soka Gakkai leaders like Ikeda meet with foreign leaders, they are increasing the web of understanding between Japanese and other peoples. [1]

It is difficult to judge the importance of any of these meetings outside the realm of Gakkai propaganda except that Ikeda (in his travels) has played a direct role in establishing numerous Soka Gakkai chapters abroad. Leaders of its American wing, NSA, for example, note that Ikeda's first visit to the United States in 1960 involved sessions with young members in the United States who, with his strong encouragement, began to build NSA.

One area of intense Soka Gakkai involvement abroad in recent years has been China. Gakkai leaders stress that involvement by the Soka Gakkai may have had a positive effect in improving the relationship between Japan and China. This story not only involves many undocumented claims by the Soka Gakkai, but it also reveals much about the Gakkai's self-image and its actual power in Japanese politics.

## Japan and China

Several years ago Tagawa Seiichi, a conservative Japanese politician and longtime advocate of Sino-Japanese friendship, wrote an article on postwar Sino-Japanese relationships. He correctly pointed out that Japan had no official ties with the Beijing regime between 1952 and 1972. However, tenuous ties were maintained through various nongovernmental and cultural exchange groups that sought to promote closer relations between the two nations with the tacit permission of both governments. There were many visits to China by cultural groups, politicians from Japan's ruling Liberal-Democratic Party and other parties, and businessmen. These early contacts set the stage for the re-establishment of official relations, which began with the visit to China of former Prime Minister Tanaka Kakuei in September, 1972.[2]

While Mr. Tagawa is justifiably proud of the role that he and other Japanese politicians played in maintaining contacts with China during a very troubled period, he makes no mention of the role the Soka Gakkai and the Komeito, and their leader, Ikeda Daisaku, may have played in bringing China and Japan closer together. Indeed, the Soka Gakkai and Komeito both claim that Ikeda, the Gakkai's third president, was the key person in the re-establishment of Sino-Japanese ties.[3]

While some analysts claim that the Soka Gakkai is guilty of gross exaggeration, it is clear that there is a long and established friendship between the leaders of both the Soka Gakkai and the government of China. This relationship is not without significance in Japan. The Soka Gakkai still exerts great power in the political realm with its influence over the Komeito, which typically has the support of about ten percent of the electorate and fifty seats in the Japanese Diet. There is evidence that the Chinese seek to reach a large and sympathetic audience in Japan through the Soka Gakkai, to influence political events in Japan by making use of Ikeda's political clout, and to use Ikeda as a handy way of communicating with the Japanese public. It also seems likely that the Soka Gakkai worked as a direct intermediary between the Tanaka government and the Chinese in 1971-72. If the Soka Gakkai and its political party helped to establish links between the Chinese and the Tanaka government at that time, then one can say that the private diplomacy of the Soka Gakkai and Komeito is not without influence.

On the surface, the Soka Gakkai's friendship with China seems like a very strange relationship. Japan's largest active Buddhist organization, the Soka Gakkai, whose professed goal is the active propagation of its version of Nichiren Buddhism throughout the world, has become an intimate friend of a Communist government, which in theory disdains religion of any kind. Yet, since 1974, there have been numerous visits to China by Soka Gakkai officials, visits to Sika Gakkai headquarters in Tokyo by leading Chinese officials, and many cultural and educational exchanges between the two parties.

The formal relationship between the Soka Gakkai and the Chinese dates back to 1974, when Ikeda made the first of his six trips to China. But it has deeper roots. The Soka Gakkai argues that its interest in China dates back at least to 1968 when Ikeda made a well-publicized statement at the September 8th General

156

Meeting of the Gakkai's Student Division.[4] Ikeda himself notes that his concern for China dates back to World War II when his older brother was killed there in action.[5] Ikeda feels that one way to make amends for the death of his brother, as well as for the others who died in China, is to see that there is never again a war between China and Japan. In his 1968 talk, Ikeda stressed that Japan should recognize the Beijing regime, that Japan should work actively for China's admission to the United Nations, and that China should be invited to play a more active role in international trade and commerce. Ikeda also urged that top Chinese and Japanese officials should get together immediately to begin working for closer relations.[6]

A number of leading Soka Gakkai and Komeito officials believe that Ikeda's statement was one of the initial steps leading to the development of an atmosphere more conducive to the start of reconciliation talks between China and Japan. They feel that Ikeda's "courageous declaration" came at a time when relations between China and Japan had declined due to the Cultural Revolution and Vietnam War. Promising talks and tentative steps toward trade in the 1950s and early 1960s had ended in general failure, and the attitude of the Sato administration towards the Beijing regime was "write negative." At the same time "the Chinese were being consumed by the Cultural Revolution and had developed a negative attitude towards foreigners due to the Vietnam War."[7]

The Soka Gakkai asserts that Ikeda's 1968 plea for a "Golden Bridge for Peace" was the essential catalyst that began the process of accommodation between Japan and China. Ikeda has stressed that there are times when politicians cannot act and when individuals or private organizations behaving in a responsible and productive manner can make important initiatives.[8] According to one leading soka Gakkai official:

> It is hard to gauge the initial effect of this proposal. Because of its internal turmoil, China was not ready to respond effectively to this proposal, but it was reported in the Chinese press at the time. The important result of Ikeda's move is that it started a groundswell of opinion among the Japanese people in favor of better relations with China. Up until then the influential Japanese had been afraid to express any sentiments favoring improved ties with China, but after Ikeda had made his suggestion and had endured public ridicule, some who had been afraid to talk until then began themselves urging normalization of ties.[9]

Their sentiments were held by all Soka Gakkai officials I interviewed in the summer of 1984.

It was most difficult to assess the Soka Gakkai's claims. Ikeda's views were well known at the time and, in essence, became the China policy of the Komeito.[10] There were no other Soka Gakkai initiatives before the Nixon administration in 1971 stunned the world with the announcement that Henry Kissinger had arranged for the President to make a state visit to China in 1972. During that same year the Chinese had initiated their "Ping-Pong" diplomacy by inviting members of the United States Ping-Pong team to visit China. There was, however, an official Komeito mission to China from June 15 to July 6, 1971 that went for the purpose of increasing contacts with the Chinese and creating means for communication with them. There were two Komeito missions in the spring and summer of 1972 just prior to the September Sino-Japanese declaration of Peace and Friendship.[11]

One young and prominent journalist, Tsukamoto Akira, who is a specialist on the Komeito and who for a decade has covered the Diet affairs of the opposition parties for a nationwide television

network, said in 1984 that the Komeito acted in effect as a go-
between for the Tanaka government and the Chinese and thus
played a crucial role in bringing the two countries together.[12]
Tsukamoto stated that to this day Ikeda and Tanaka are close
friends, that they have performed valuable services for each other
in the past, and that their relationship of friendship and cooperation
continues. It is a matter of public record that Tanaka played an
important role in establishing a peace pact between the
Komeito/Soka Gakkai and the Japan Communist Party in 1975.[13]
According to Tsukamoto, Tanaka was willing to do this on behalf
of Ikeda as a payment for Ikeda's help in arranging contacts with
the Chinese through the Komeito.

Komeito officials agree with Tsukamoto. Yano Junya,
Chairman of the Komeito and a member of the Diet, confirmed the
Komeito's role as an intermediary between the Tanaka and the
Chinese, but advised: "We played an important role, but we were
not mere messenger-boys. We played an important advisory
role.[14] Another prominent Soka Gakkai official stated:

> The Soka Gakkai and its ally, the Komeito, did much
> to get the Japanese and Chinese together in the
> structuring of the Chinese-Japanese Peace Treaty.
> The Komeito worked directly on the principles
> enunciated earlier by Ikeda. Thus, Ikeda's and the
> Gakkai's role in bringing the two nations closer
> together is very important.[15]

It is not very easy to otherwise document the Soka Gakkai's
role in helping to improve Sino-Japanese relations. I have found
no other documentary evidence of this, and other scholars in the
field have been a bit skeptical. On the other hand, there is the
testimony of the Soka Gakkai and the Komeito, as well as a
verification form a key journalist, Tsukamoto Akira. There is also
the fact that Ikeda has made many trips to China and that a history

of a very close relationship between the Chinese and the Soka Gakkai/Komeito exists today. In any case, there is little evidence that the Soka Gakkai played any key role prior to 1971. Ikeda's 1968 statement is a bit early to have had much effect; however, he may have set a precedent by coming out as a friend at a time when relations were strained. Also, the Komeito made recognition of China as part of its China policy before 1971 so that when it came time to improve Sino-Japanese relations, the Chinese may have been more willing to work closely with a known friend. A more tangible point is that Ikeda's ideas became the official China policy of the Komeito. On the other hand, Soka Gakkai documents show no noticeable activity vis-a-vis China between 1968-72.

At the very least, Ikeda's declaration allowed the Gakkai to set its eyes on a relationship with the Chinese and to start preparing for such a relationship. It could later show the Chinese that its interest in them had historical roots, which is something that the Chinese value deeply. It is hardly coincidental that the first Gakkai missions to China began in early 1974 and resulted in two visits that year. Soka Gakkai officials admit that both sides regarded each other with a certain degree of suspicion on these early visits, but the Chinese received the Soka Gakkai with a great deal of hospitality and arranged meetings between Ikeda, Chou En-lai and Deng Xiaoping.

The second Gakkai mission in December 1974 also achieved some tangible results. Sizable donations of books were made to Beijing University, and Ikeda personally agreed to act as a guarantor for Chinese students interested in coming to Soka University for study. In April, 1975, six Chinese students entered Soka University, becoming the first Chinese students to study in Japan in a very long time. After their graduation, these students returned to important jobs as translators for the Chinese government.  When Ikeda returned to Peking in 1984, he found that the translator for Hu Yaobang was one of the first Soka graduates.

There were other Soka Gakkai missions to China in 1975, 1978, 1980 and 1984.  On these trips Gakkai officials became known and respected in China, and they developed friendly relationships with a number of influential Chinese political, cultural, and social leaders.  In turn a number of Chinese political and cultural delegations have been greeted by Soka Gakkai officials in Tokyo, and some Chinese artists have performed at Soka University.  Delegations from the Soka Gakkai's Youth, Doctor's, Education, Women's and Men's Divisions have visited China on more than one occasion.  There has also been a growing number of exchanges between students and faculty of both Beijing and Soka Universities.

The strength and warmth of this relationship is symbolized by the success of a visit of Ikeda, along with a large delegation of Gakkai officials, to China in early June, 1984.  Two of the highlights of the trip were a ninety minute meeting with Communist Party leader Hu Yaobang and the awarding of an honorary professorship to Ikeda by Beijing University.

The dialogue between Ikeda and Hu covered a wide range of topics.[16]  Hu suggested to Ikeda that the Chinese are very interested in the concept of nuclear disarmament and want the US and USSR to work more assiduously to ease tensions.  Hu noted that he would like to see the Olympics held in China in the 1990s, that there should be wider trade links between the Chinese and Japanese, and that, in his opinion, the North Koreans did not harbor antagonistic feelings towards the Japanese, a conclusion reached by Hu on a recent trip to North Korea.  Hu stressed that the U.S. and the two Korean states should get together in the near future in an attempt to ease tensions on the Korean peninsula.

Ikeda was awarded an honorary professorship at Beijing University, a rare honor. On that occasion Ikeda delivered a long talk entitled "The Royal Road to Peace" in which he urged the Chinese to adopt a policy of resolute action to help the other super-powers ease tensions.[17]

It is interesting to speculate why the Chinese have lavished so much attention on the Soka Gakkai, and whether they take Ikeda and the Soka Gakkai seriously. Ikeda is deeply revered by millions of Soka Gakkai members in Japan, as well as by the officialdom of both the Gakkai and the Komeito. The Chinese must be well aware of Ikeda's political power at home and the massive following that he has in the Soka Gakkai. They have invited him to China on six occasions in a decade, have allowed him to meet and establish relationships with leading officials such as Hu Yaobang, have given him a very prestigious award from Beijing University, and have given his visits broad coverage in their press. Soka Gakkai officials said that there was good television coverage of Ikeda's meeting with Hu Yaobang and his speech at Beijing University. This is clear evidence of the fact that the Chinese take their relationship with Ikeda very seriously.

China desires closer ties with Japan, and Ikeda is an important link. The Chinese are historically reluctant to work with people that they do not know well and place a premium on long term relationships with influential foreigners. A good example of this is their desire to maintain a lasting relationship with Richard Nixon despite his disgrace in the United States. Ikeda is a known figure with influence in certain circles in Japan who has gained the trust of the Chinese. It probably does not matter much to the Chinese that Ikeda has been vilified by the Japanese press because of his so-called involvement in a series of recent scandals. Ikeda may be past his prime in Japan, but he still has tremendous respect and influence within the Soka Gakkai and Komeito.

The Chinese also like to use their meetings with influential foreigners as a means of conveying certain messages to the outside world. Thus, it is most convenient for them to have frequent meetings with people like Ikeda, especially when the Chinese believe that he wields significant political power in Japan.

Aside from political contact, Ikeda and the Soka Gakkai provide the Chinese and Japanese with important cultural and educational exchange programs. One Soka Gakkai official points out that the Soka Gakkai cultural missions to China have had some meaningful results.[18] A recent visit by representatives of the Gakkai's Doctor's Division brought some Japanese doctors into contact with their peers in China for the first time. As a result of a tour of a group of Soka Gakkai officials interested in cooking, the first Chinese-run Japanese restaurant was opened recently in Beijing. In addition, the Gakkai has donated many books and Soka University has accepted Chinese students. These developments, however minor, are important to Chinese leaders in their efforts to improve relationships with Japan.

The Chinese are also apparently convinced that Japan, which is closely tied with both the Chinese and the West, can play an important role as an intermediary and stabilizer in areas of conflict. The Chinese believe in putting a strong emphasis on personal relationships and using the Soka Gakkai as a means of reaching several million Japanese: They know full well that a friendly reception to Ikeda will strongly influence the millions of Gakkai members in Japan. This was demonstrated by the full coverage given to Ikeda's trip by the Soka Gakkai press, even though this event was virtually ignored by other Japanese newspapers. The Gakkai's Seikyo Shimbun itself has 4.5 million readers.

The Soka Gakkai also has much to gain from these China missions. It hopes it can get some valuable publicity and prestige by having its leaders meet with influential Chinese. The hope is that the meetings with the Chinese leaders will add to the prestige of its own peace movement and give validity to its assertion that its religion is indeed to be taken seriously as a vehicle for the attainment of world brotherhood. Gakkai officials also take pride in the fact that their movement has at least in some small ways helped to ease the once-tense relations between these former enemies.[19]

Thus, it is clear that the Soka Gakkai feels that it has been an important link in establishing ties with the Chinese. There can be no doubt that its role in helping to link the Tanaka government with the Chinese in early 1970s may well have been critically important in cementing Sino-Japanese ties. However, one must question the usefulness to the Japanese of the Soka Gakkai-Chinese ties today; unless, of course, the ties with Tanaka and the LDP are as important now as they were during the Tanaka period.

Is personal diplomacy by such groups as the Soka Gakkai productive? If they are working on behalf of a government, then Gakkai leaders may gain outside attention and support; however, if they are working on their own, leaders will most likely gain critical publicity and support only within their own movement. Because there are localized benefits from continued contact between the Chinese and the Soka Gakkai, Ikeda will probably keep on making his trips, but the Soka Gakkai's role as a major "well-digger" is probably finished.

# NOTES

[1]Akiya interview in Tokyo on 20 March 1987.

[2]Tagawa Seiichi, "Don't Forget the Well-Diggers," in _Japan Quarterly_, XXVI (1979), p. 18.

[3]Interview with Daisaku Ikeda at Soka University, July 15, 1984.

[4]"Chugoku to Yuko Koryu no rekishi." (History of friendly exchange with China). Soka Gakkai document published in 1984.

[5]Ikeda interview.

[6]"Chukoku to yuko koryu no rekishi," pp. 4-16.

[7]Interview with Zhou Jinxiong, International Bureau, the Soka Gakkai. In Tokyo on June 17, 1984. He was Ikeda's official translator in China.

[8]Ibid.

[9]Interview with Ueda Masaichi, Soksz Gakkai Vice President, in Tokyo on June 12, 1984.

[10]James White, _The Soka Gakkai and Mass Society_ (Stanford, 1970), p. 147.

[11]"Kokusai Koryu-haken." (International Comings and Goings). Komeito document published in 1983.

[12]Interviews with Tsukamoto Akira in Tokyo on 14 and 30 July, 1984.

[13]See Danile Metraux, "The Religious and Social Philosophy of the Soka Gakkai," (Unpublished doctoral dissertation). Columbia University, 1978, pp. 262-63.

[14]Interview with Yano Junya, Diet Building, Tokyo, 30 July 1984.

[15]Interview with Aoki Tooru, Soka Gakkai Vice President, and Matsuoka Osamu, Gen. Mgt. Ed. Seikyo Press, in Tokyo on 20 June 1984.

[16]Seikyo Shimbun, June 5-8, 1984, and Asahi Shimbun, June 7, 1984.

[17]Ibid.

[18]Zhou Interview.

[19]Ibid.

# CHAPTER 10

## CONCLUDING NOTES

An important theme of the Soka Gakkai movement is _Rissho Ankoku Ron_. In this thirteenth century work, a Japanese Buddhist monk looked at all of the doom and destruction going on about him and decided that the cause was the fact that his countrymen were following false religious doctrines. They were ignoring the truth of the _Lotus Sutra_ and were living in misery. Their distress was ample evidence in support of the Buddhist idea of _mappo_, which states that man is in misery because he does not follow the true doctrines of the Buddha.

Nichiren blamed "false priests" for tricking the people, and he blamed the government for supporting these vagabond priests. Nichiren petitioned the government to stop patronizing the priests. He realized that direct political action was necessary and was willing to be a martyr to his cause since he was so very convinced of the truth of his beliefs. He saw a wonderful Buddhaland on this earth if all mankind would chant the _daimoku_ of the _Lotus Sutra_.

Today, the Soka Gakkai considers itself to be the true practitioner of Nichiren's doctrines. It accepts Nichiren's admonition that mankind in the twentieth century still is in the age of _mappo_, but it argues that conditions have deteriorated. We are now even further away from the teachings of the Buddha Shakyamuni and are becoming increasingly depraved. Unless we do something to reverse current trends, mankind will destroy itself in nuclear war. Soka Gakkai leaders caution that although Japan is enjoying great prosperity in the 1980s, Japan today is spiritually dead. Its citizens work hard, but they have no purpose or direction in life. They are unhappy and do not know how to lead more fulfilling lives.[1]

The Soka Gakkai offers World War II as a case study of the truth of Nichiren's teachings. Japan was destroyed in the war because it turned to a false religion (Shinto) for help and because leaders of the Soka Gakkai, who adamantly opposed the war, were put in jail. The punishment for Japan was the atomic bombing of Hiroshima and Nagasaki.

As horrible as World War II was, however, it was not nearly as bad as nuclear war in the future will be. World War II was only a small example of how horrible mappo can be. If mankind fails to heed this warning, then all of mankind will perish and human history will come to an end--the striking eschatological message of the Soka Gakkai. Even if this nuclear holocaust does not take place, man is afflicted by a vast array of problems including apathy, pollution, high crime rates, drugs, and so on, which combine to make life difficult for all concerned.[2]

But just as the eschatological message of Christians and Jews contains hope for a triumph of good over evil, the Soka Gakkai and its parent sect, Nichiren Shoshu, claim that Nichiren, who is said to be the true saving Buddha of mappo, left a very important mandala, the Daigohonzon. By praying to this mandala, which is the essence of life and the embodiment of Nichiren the Buddha, mankind will experience a massive series of individual "human revolutions," which will change a debased world view to the far better one by the improvement of individual karmas. The resulting "human revolutions," will supposedly bring about the creation of a Buddha land on earth.

The Soka Gakkai, which has built a membership of several million followers in Japan and several hundred thousand abroad, has also been active politically both at home and abroad. It does not seek to join the government; like Nichiren, it seems far more content with the role of a hard-driving gadfly. Its politicians on the Diet and elsewhere, along with its religious leaders, have been among the severest critics of the government, although in at least one instance it has worked informally for the Japanese government to promote better relations with the People's Republic of China.

Its accomplishments are impressive. It has built a strong and devoted national and international following. Many of its members feel that the movement has had a very profound and positive effect on their lives and attribute much of their personal success to what they have gained through worship and membership. It is difficult to judge happiness from the outside, but most Gakkai members I have encountered seem far more satisfied with their lives than do most Japanese as a whole.

It is difficult to chart the future of the Soka Gakkai. It is more than a mere one-issue pressure group--it is very able in its organization and has stands on a variety of issues and problems both religious and secular. The very successful organizational structure of the Gakkai allows it to appeal to men and women alike and to people from all walks of life. Somehow it manages to weld all of these diverse elements into a cohesive group. The odds are that the Soka Gakkai will not grow much more beyond its current membership--that rather it will attempt mainly to strengthen its existing programs.

A real crisis will come when Ikeda Daisaku passes from the scene. He is idolized by many members. In many publications one finds endless pictures and articles about Ikeda as if the Gakkai were little more than an Ikeda cult. A major portion of the Gakkai Fuji Art Museum near the head temple at Taiseki-ji contains photographs by Ikeda as if he were the only artist in the world who mattered. This cult-like behavior is detrimental to the movement as a whole because it calls attention away from the work and contributions of other outside leaders. This adulation for Ikeda from within the Soka Gakkai gives some outside observers the impression that the true object of worship is not Nichiren or his mandalas, but Ikeda himself. This tendency is certainly not healthy. In person, Ikeda is a gentle and rather unassuming gentleman, but he must be encouraged to urge members and Soka Gakkai publications to devote more attention to other aspects of Gakkai life. There is a whole generation of very able Gakkai leaders on the horizon who need more attention. Otherwise, when Ikeda dies or is unable to lead the Gakkai some day in the future, Gakkai members will have difficulty in adjusting to new leaders.

## NOTES

[1] Interview with President Akiya, 20 March 1987.

[2] Ibid.

# GLOSSARY

(Note: These terms are arranged by subject
matter.)

**Nichiren Shoshu** - A sect of Buddhism which regards Nichiren Daishonin as its founder and Nikko Shonin as his immediate successor. It considers itself the guardian of the teaching of true Buddhism. Its head temple is Taiseki-ji in Shizuoka Prefecture. The basis of its doctrine is the belief that Nichiren Daishonin is the original Buddha who appeared in the Latter Day of the Law, and the Three Great Secret Laws (q.v.), which include the invocation or daimoku Nam-myoho-renge-kyo (q.v.). The sect considers that it was founded by Nichiren Daishonin in the 5th year of the Kencho era (1253). Its teachings were given definite form in the 2nd year of the Koan era (1279) when Nichiren Daishonin inscribed the Dai-Gohonzon (q.v.) of the high sanctuary of true Buddhism, a mandala that enables all persons to attain buddhahood. After the demise of Nichiren Daishonin in 1282, Nikko Shonin succeeded him as the second high priest of the sect, and in the 3rd year of the Shoo era (1290) founded Taiseki-ji in the foothills of Mount Fuji to act as the head temple of the sect. He was in time succeeded by the third high priest Nichimoku, the fourth high priest Nichido, and so on for a period of some seven hundred years down to the present, during which the doctrines of Nichiren Daishonin have been guarded and transmitted by the successive leaders of the sect. The sect is presently headed by Nikken Shonin, the 67th in the direct line of succession.

**Nichiren (1222-1282)** - A Japanese Buddhist leader who is regarded by the Nichiren Shoshu (q.v.) as the original Buddha who appeared in the Latter Day of the Law. He was born in the village of Kominato in Tojo in Awa Province (present day Kominato Township, Chiba Prefecture, Japan). His childhood name was Zennichimaro. At the age of 12 he entered a nearby temple called Seicho-ji, where he received an education, and at the age of 16 formally became a member of the priesthood, taking the name Zesho-bo Rencho. After traveling to Kamakura, Mt. Hiei, and other centers of Buddhism in Japan in order to further his studies, he announced the founding of his own sect based on the Lotus Sutra on the 28th day of the 4th month of Kencho 5 (1253).

He took up residence in a small hut in a place called Matsubagayatsu in the city of Kamakura and devoted himself to the spreading of his teachings.  On the 16th day of the 7th month of Bun'o 1 (1260) he finished writing his treatise entitled <u>Rissho Ankoku Ron</u> (On Securing the Peace of the Land through the Propagation of True Buddhism), which he submitted to Hojo Tokiyori, the most influential man in the Kamakura government, urging him to take faith in the true Buddhist teachings set forth by Nichiren in order to insure the peace and safety of the nation.

He continued to spread his teachings despite an attack upon his residence at Matsubagayatsu by followers of opposing sects and a period of exile in the Izu Peninsula brought about by the charges of his opponents.  On the 12th day of the 9th month of Bun'ei 8 (1271), he was charged with treason and came close to being executed in an incident known as the Tatsunokuchi Persecution, and at this time he revealed his true identity as the original Buddha of the Latter Day of the Law.

He was sentenced to exile in the island of Sado in the Japan Sea.  After several years of hardship, he was pardoned in Bun'ei 11 (1274), and thereafter retired to a remote area at Mount Minobu in the present Yamanashi Prefecture.  There, on the 12th day of the 10th month of Koan 2 (1279), he inscribed the Dai-Gohonzon of the high sanctuary of true Buddhism as the object of worship whereby all people for all time would be able to attain Buddhahood.  In the 5th year of Koan (1282), he designated Nikko Shonin as his successor, entrusting all his teachings to him, and passed away at the home of Ikegami Munenaka, an important lay follower, at Ikegami in Musashi Province.  His voluminous writings include the <u>Rissho Ankoku Ron</u> already mentioned above, the <u>Kaimoku Sho</u>  or The Opening of the Eyes, the <u>Kanjin no Honzon Sho</u> or The True Object of Worship, and many others.

**Nichiren Daishonin** - "Shonin" can be interpreted as "sage," or "saint."   "Daishonin," or "Great Sage" is used by the Nichiren Shoshu as a mark of respect for Nichiren, whom it honors as the Buddha of the Latter Day of the Law.

**<u>Rissho Ankoku Ron</u>** (On Securing the Peace of the Land through the Propagation of True Buddhism) - An admonitory treatise completed by Nichiren Daishonin on the 16th day of the 7th month of Bun'o (1260) and presented to Hojo Tokiyori, the most influential leader in the Kamakura government at the time.  In it he argues that the natural disasters, famines and epidemic that plagued Japan at that period were caused by the fact that the people of the time had turned their backs upon the true Buddhist teachings and were putting their faith in evil doctrines.  Among the particularly mentioned the Nembutsu teachings of Honen. If all support for these heretical doctrines were cut off and people put their faith in true Buddhism, he stated, disasters and calamities would cease and an era of peace and paradise on earth would ensue. But if the nation failed to put faith in the correct teachings, he warned that Japan would inevitably suffer the two disasters of internal revolt and invasion from abroad. He consequently strongly urged that the authorities take immediate steps to adopt the correct teachings of Buddhism as expounded by the Daishonin. Hojo Tokiyori failed to heed these warnings. Soon after, as the Daishonin had predicted, an internal revolt broke out within the Hojo family and Japan was attacked by Mongol forces from overseas.

**Kanjin no Honzon Sho**  (The True Object of Worship) - A treatise written by Nichiren Daishonin in Bun'ei 10 (1273), when he was in exile in the island of Sado. It cites various sutras and treatises to make clear that the object of worship as revealed by the Daishonin represents the ultimate Law embodied in the Lotus Sutra. For this reason it is often stated that this treatise reveals the object of worship in terms of the Law. The treatise further explains that by embracing the object of worship and chanting the invocation or daimoku Nammyoho-renge-kyo, all persons can attain lives that are replete with compassion and wisdom. This treatise ranks with the Kaimoku Sho as one of the most important of the Daishonin's writings.

**Kaimoku Sho**  (The Opening of the Eyes) - A treatise written by Nichiren Daishonin in Bun'ei 1 (1272), when he was in exile on Sado Island. In it the Daishonin cites the passages in the Lotus Sutra that predict that two thousand years after the passing of Shakyamuni Buddha, the Bodhisattvas of the Earth will appear and devote themselves to propagating the teachings of the Lotus Sutra, and will at that time meet with the various trials and persecutions. The Daishonin points out that he himself is carrying out such activities and enduring such persecutions. He goes on to make clear his own view that Bodhisattva Jogyo, the leader of the Bodhisattvas of the Earth, is in fact the original Buddha who appears in the Latter Day of the Law in order to bring enlightenment to all persons. For this reason it is frequently stated that this treatise reveals the object of worship in terms of the Person, i.e., the original Buddha of the Latter Day of the Law. It ranks with the Kanjin no Honzon Sho as one of the most important of the Daishonin's writings.

**Mappo** (The Latter Day of the Law) - One is a set of three terms used to designate successive periods which the Buddhist Law or teachings go through in respect to their relative effectiveness. The three terms are shobo, the period of the Correct Law, also known as the Former Day of the Law; zobo, the period of the Imitative Law, or the Middle Day of the Law; and mappo, the End of the Law or the Latter Day of the Law. During the period known as mappo, the third period following the deaths of Shakyamuni Buddha, though the Buddhist teachings are still in existence, the people of the time, because of the relative weakness and impurity of their life force, are unable to attain Buddhahood through these teachings. There are varying theories as to when the period of mappo will occur, though the most common view holds that it will begin 2,000 years after Shakyamuni's passing. According to the Lotus Sutra, in the period of mappo, or the Latter Day of the Law, the Bodhisattva of the Earth, who is in fact the Buddha of the Latter Day of the Law, will appear to propagate the essence of the Lotus Sutra.

**The Lotus Sutra** - Forty-two years after Shakyamuni Buddha attained enlightenment, he declared in the Muryogi Sutra: "For the past more than forty years, I have not yet revealed the truth." In the eight years that followed, he then proceeded to preach the Lotus Sutra, referred to in Japanese as the Hokekyo, at a place called Eagle Peak. Shakyamuni himself stated that this was "the highest" among all his teachings. The Lotus Sutra makes clear that certain groups of people which in earlier sutras had been declared incapable of attaining Buddhahood, such as persons in the realms of shomon and engaku or evildoers and women, could in fact do so--in other words, that all persons without exception can gain enlightenment. There are various Chinese translations of the Lotus Sutra, but the most accurate and widely used is that in 8 volumes and 28 chapters by Kumarajiva entitled Myoho-renge-kyo.

**Three Great Secret Laws** - The Three Great Secret Laws, known in Japanese as Sandaihiho, consist of the object of worship of true Buddhism (Hommon no honzon), the invocation or daimoku of true Buddhism (Hommon no daimoku), and the high sanctuary of true Buddhism (Hommon no kaidan). They constitute the core of the Buddhism taught by Nichiren Daishonin. Hommon or true Buddhism here refers not to the teachings of Shakyamuni Buddha but to those revealed exclusively by Nichiren Daishonin. The object of worship is the Dai-Gohonzon which the Daishonin inscribed on the 12th day of the 10th month of Koan 2 (1279) to serve as the object of worship in the high sanctuary of true Buddhism. The daimoku of true Buddhism consists of the invocation Nammyoho-renge-kyo which one chants with faith in the object of worship. The high sanctuary of true Buddhism is the designated place where one chants the daimoku to the object of worship.

**Namn-myoho-renge-kyo** - This term has the following meanings: (1) It represents the object or content of the enlightenment achieved by Nichiren Daishonin, the ultimate Law underlying the universe and all life. (2) Because this fundamental Law is made manifest through the activities of Nichiren Daishonin, the Buddha of the Latter Day of the Law, the term refers to the life force of the Daishonin himself. (3) It represents the core or essence of the Buddhism which lies hidden but inherent in the Juryo chapter of the Lotus Sutra, and is the fundamental cause or means by which all Buddhas are enabled to achieve enlightenment. (4) Nichiren Daishonin inscribed the words Nam-myoho-renge-kyo to serve as the Dai-Gohonzon or ultimate object of worship for the high sanctuary of true Buddhism. (5) All persons everywhere in the world in the Latter Day of the Law, by taking faith in the Dai-Gohonzon and chanting the invocation Nam-myoho-renge-kyo, can attain Buddhahood.

**Gohonzon** - The word honzon in Japanese means an object of worship, something to which one pays profound respect. Go is a particle that is prefixed to other words to indicate honor or respect. The term honzon is employed as an equivalent of the Sanskrit in mandala. In ancient India, the word mandala referred originally to an area of ground marked off in the form of a square or a circle and used in conducting worship services to the various Buddhas. Later the term came to mean a diagrammatic picture or representation of Buddhas and Buddhist deities that was used as an object of worship. Nichiren Daishonin defined the ultimate Law contained in the Lotus Sutra as Nam-myoho-renge-kyo and embodied it in the form of a mandala or Gohonzon to be the object of worship for all persons in the Latter Day of the Law.

**Dai-Gohonzon** - The mandala which Nichiren Daishonin inscribed on the 12th day of the 10th month of Koan 2 (1279) to be the object of worship for the high sanctuary of true Buddhism. Among the numerous mandalas inscribed by the Daishonin, this represents the ultimate one, the inscribing of which was the purpose of his advent in the world. Because it is dedicated to all persons of the entire continent of Jambudvipa, that is, of the entire world, it is often referred to as the Dai-Gohonzon for all the world. It constitutes the object of worship of true Buddhism,one of the Three Great Secret Laws which make up the core of the

Daishonin's teachings. It is presently enshrined in the Sho-Hondo or Grand Main Temple of Taiseki-ji, the head temple of Nichiren Shoshu in Shizuoka Prefecture.

**Shakubuku** - The practice of Buddhism must embrace two types of activities, the individual's own practice of the teachings, and the efforts which he or she makes to spread the teachings to others. Shakubuku is a term designating one of the two methods used to propagate the teachings, and refers to the efforts one makes to awaken others to errors in their outlook upon life or to the mistakes in the teachings of other sects of Buddhism and to lead them to a faith in true Buddhism for the sake of their own happiness. Buddhist doctrine condemns a self-centered style of life that seeks only for the happiness of the individual. Instead, it emphasizes the importance of positive actions that are designed to rescue others from the cares and troubles that beset them. It teaches that only when we engage in such positive and practical application of the teachings can we develop the full potential for compassion and wisdom that is present in ourselves. In this sense, shakubuku is one of the most important of all Buddhist practices because it is aimed at securing happiness both for oneself and for others.

**Gongyo** - The most fundamental and important practice for believers in Nichiren Shoshu. Religious practice is of two kinds, that which is directed to others (keta). Gongyo belongs to the former category. Twice a day, once in the morning and again at evening, the believer sits in formal posture facing the Gohonzon, recites from the Lotus Sutra and chants the invocation. The sections of the sutra recited are of the Hoben and Juryo chapters, which constitute the heart of the Lotus Sutra. The invocation of daimoku consists of the words Nam-myoho-renge-kyo. Through this practice, one develops the life force that is innate within him to the highest degree, so that it becomes fully endowed with compassion and wisdom, and employs it to create for himself a life of unending happiness and blessing.

**Zadankai** - Zadankai or "discussion meeting" is a term used for gatherings of small numbers of Soka Gakkai members who get together to study and deepen their faith, mainly through the medium of discussion. Ordinarily the groups consist of from four to five to several dozen persons, Soka Gakkai members and their friends, who gather at the home of one of the members to study the Buddhist teachings of Nichiren Daishonin and instruct one another in the practice of their faith. The meetings also provide an opportunity for participants to talk about various problems in their daily lives and to deepen their faith in that way. The meetings thus provide a means for spreading religious understanding among the general populace. Since the earliest days of the Soka Gakkai, discussion meetings have played a key role in the propagation of the faith, and they continue to be one of the most important activities for members, who customarily attend such meetings once a month in their neighborhood.

**Tozan** - Tozan, which means literally "climbing the mountain," is a term used to refer to a visit to Taiseki-ji, the head temple of Nichiren Shoshu located in the foothills of Mount Fuji in Fujinomiya City, Shizuoka Prefecture. Taiseki-ji was founded by Nikko Shonin, the second high priest of Nichiren Shoshu and the inheritor of Nichiren Daishonin's Buddhism. In the seven hundred years since its founding, it has faithfully guarded and handed down the orthodox tradition of the Daishonin's teachings. Within its grounds is the Sho-Hondo or Grand Main Temple, in which is enshrined the Dai-Gohonzon or ultimate object of worship of the high sanctuary of true Buddhism, inscribed by Nichiren Daishonin on the 12th day of the 10th month of Koan 2 (1279). The main purpose in visiting the temple is to enter the Sho-Hondo, worship the Dai-Gohonzon, and pray for the expiation of any offenses one may have committed against true Buddhism, and for the peace of the world and one's own happiness.

**Kyogaku** - The term Kyogaku or "study of the teachings" refers to study of the Gosho, the collected treatises, letters and other writings of Nichiren Daishonin for the purpose of gaining a better understanding of the doctrines of the Daishonin's Buddhism and deepening one's faith and religious practice. The Daishonin in his Shoho Jisso Sho (On the True Entity of All Phenomena) states: "Exert yourself in the two ways of practice and study. Without practice and study, there can be no Buddhism." From this we can see that study of the doctrine, along with such practical religious activities as shakubuku, constitutes one of the most important aspects of Buddhist practice.

**Nembutsu** - In general usage, the term is used to refer to shomho nembutsu, a devotional practice in which one fixes one's thoughts upon the Buddha Amida and recites the formula Namu Amida Butsu. In Japan the nembutsu practice was advocated by Honen (1133-1212), who founded the sect known as the Jodo or Pure Land sect.

**Soka Kyoiku Gakkai** - Soka Kyoiku Gakkai (Value-Creating Education Society) is the name by which Soka Gakkai was known during the period from its founding in Showa 5 (1930) until Showa

20 (1945), when the Pacific War ended. The organization was created by Makiguchi Tsunesaburo, its first president, and Toda Josei, the second president. Since Makiguchi was an educator by profession, the original objective of the group was to work for educational reforms, but it gradually became transformed into an organization of believers in the Buddhism expounded by Nichiren Daishonin whose purpose was to work for the propagation of Nichiren Daishonin's teachings. In Showa 16 (1941), it began issuing a publication entitled Kachi Sozo (Creation of Values), and the membership grew until it numbered over 3,000 persons.

**Makiguchi Tsunesaburo (1871-1944)** - First president of soka Gakkai. After graduating from Hokkaido Normal School, he became a teacher and later the principal of an elementary school in Tokyo. He was also known as a geographer. He evolved a theory of value creation based on the concepts of beauty, benefit and goodness, and advocated a system of progressive reforms in education. In Showa 3 (1928) he became a follower of the Nichiren Shoshu sect of Buddhism, and in Showa 5 (1930) established an organization called Soka Kyoiku Gakkai (Value-Creating Education Society), which later became known as Soka Gakkai. In Showa 18 (1943), after the outbreak of the Pacific War, he was arrested because he opposed the efforts of the militaristic government of the time to impose restrictions upon religious activity, and died in prison the following year. His published works include Jinsei Chirigaku (Human Geography) and Soka Kyoikugaku Taikei (Value-Creating Pedagogy).

**Toda Josei (1900-1958)** - Second president of Soka Gakkai. After graduating from Chu University he became a primary school teacher. While in that post, he met Makiguchi Tsunesaburo and became his disciple. In Showa 3 (1928) he became a follower of Nichiren Shoshu. In Showa 5 (1930) he joined with Makiguchi in founding Soka Kyoiku Gakkai (Value-Creating Education Society). After the outbreak of the Pacific War he was subjected to harassment for his religious beliefs by the militaristic government of the time and spent over two years in prison. He was released from prison in Showa 20 (1945), shortly before the end of the war. After changing the name to Soka Gakkai, he started to rebuild the virtually defunct organization, and in Showa 26 (1951) he became the second president. Continuing his efforts until the time of his death in Showa 33 (1958), he succeeded in building up the membership to 750,000 households. His published works include Suirishiki Shido Sanjutsu (A Deductive Approach to Teaching Arithmetic) and Ningen Kakumei (The Human Revolution).

**Ikeda Daisaku (1928-   )** - President of Soka Gakkai International
(SGI), honorary president of Soka Gakkai, head of the Nichiren
Shoshu Hokkeko.   He is a graduate of Fuji Junior college.   In
Showa 22 (1947) he joined Nichiren Shoshu and became a
disciple of Josei Toda, the second president of Soka Gakkai.   In
Showa 35 (1960) he became the third president of Soka Gakkai.
Under his energetic leadership, the organization expanded to a
membership of some 8 million households.   During this same
period he founded such organizations as the Min-on Concert
Association, Soka University, and the Komeito political party.   He
has met and held discussion with government officials and
intellectual and cultural leaders in countries throughout the world in
order to further international understanding, devoting great time
and effort to the cause of world peace.   In Showa 58 (1983) he
received the United Nations Peace Award.   His writings include
Ningen Kakumei (The Human Revolution) in 210 volumes, Choose
Life (Dialogues with Arnold Toynbee), La Nuit appelle l'aurore
(Dialogues with Rene Huyghe), and many others.

**Seikyo Shimbun** - The official newspaper of the Soka Gakkai; its
present circulation is 4.7 million.   It aims to be not only the official
publication for a single religious organization, but to follow an
editorial policy designed to represent humanity as a whole,
keeping always in mind the need to guard the sanctity of life.   With
the Buddhist teachings of Nichiren Daishonin as its keynote, it
works on a broad front to spread religious understanding among
the populace and to encourage activities that promote peace and
cultural enrichment.   The paper was founded in Showa 26 (1951).
It was originally a 2-page broadsheet that came out three times a
month, but today it is a 12-page daily.

**Obutsu myogo** - A term abbreviated from the writings of Nichiren
Daishonin and referring to a doctrine expounded by him regarding
the ideal relationship between society and religion.   The term obo
or secular law (literally, "law of the sovereign"), of which o is an
abbreviation, refers to society as a whole, including its various
political and cultural aspects, which buppo or the Buddhist Law, of
which butsu is an abbreviation, refers to the Buddhist teachings of
Nichiren Daishonin.   The term myogo indicates a state in which
two entities form a deep or fundamental unity.   According to this
doctrine, the compassion and the profound and lasting concern
for the dignity of life that are embodied in the Buddhist teachings of
Nichiren Daishonin provide the soil out of which political, economic
cultural and artistic pursuits that are truly humanistic in nature can
develop and mature.   The term refers, in other words, to the

which that Law has been thoroughly propagated through the process known as kosen-rufu.

**Ningen kakumei** - Ningen kakumei or "human revolution" was a term used by Toda Josei, the second president of Soka Gakkai, to indicate the goal which one seeks to attain through the practice of Nichiren Daishonin's Buddhism. The revolution is achieved by establishing a firm purpose in life and thereby bringing about the self-realization of the individual. Each person has within him the life force of the Buddha. Through faith, the inner life force is brought forth and given concrete form so that it can be transformed into a way of life that is characterized by compassion, wisdom and vitality. By manifesting this life force that exists in the very deepest part of the individual, the person can attain the greatest degree of fulfillment that is possible in the course of a lifetime, establishing a life of perpetual happiness and good fortune that cannot be destroyed by any outside force. The multivolume work entitled Ningen Kakumei or The Human Revolution by Ikeda Daisaku, third president of Soka Gakkai, is a fictionalized account of the life of the second president, Josei Toda. Two films were produced in Japan on the basis of this work, Ningen Kakumei or "The Human Revolution" (1973) and Zoku Ningen Kakumei or "The Human Revolution II" (1976).

**Seimeiron** - The term seimeiron or "life theory" is ordinarily used to refer in general to discussions concerning the nature of life. In Soka Gakkai,the discussion centers about the basic nature of life and life's various manifestations as seen from a Buddhist point of view. The basis of the discussion is the Buddhist doctrine of ichinen sanzen or "three thousand realms in a single life moment," and the treatment of the problem is marked by a practical approach as attention is directed to the question of how individuals ought best to live their lives.

**Buppo minshushugi** - The term buppo minshushugi or "Buddhist democracy" refers to a form of democracy that is based upon the Buddhist teachings of Nichiren Daishonin. The Daishonin's Buddhism consistently preaches the kind of true humanism, respect for life and for the individual, freedom and equality that are the cornerstones of democratic belief and practice. For this reason, it can lead to the realization of an ideal form of democracy that is founded on the Buddhist Law.

**Ningensei shakaishugi** - Ningensei shakaishugi, a term that might be translated "humanistic socialism," refers to a kind of socialism based upon the true humanism embodied in the

Buddhist thought of Nichiren Daishonin. At present the social systems of the world fall into two general groups, those that belong to the free enterprise system, and those that conform to some type of socialism. The term "humanistic socialism" refers to an effort to transcend these two types of systems and to achieve a social system that takes as its first consideration the welfare of the populace as a whole. In particular, it aims to help each of the individuals who make up the fabric of society to develop and mature his human potentialities through the spirit of compassion embodied in the Buddhist Law, to replace the confrontations in society brought about by concern for self-interest with a spirit of mutual assistance, and to realize a truly ideal type of society, one that exists on a higher dimension, in which the welfare of the individual and the prosperity of society as a whole are in perfect concord.

**Komeito** - A political party founded on November 17th, 1964 (Showa 39), with Soka Gakkai as its supporting parent organization. It is often referred to in English as the Clean Government Party. Its party platform, adopted in June 1970 (Showa 45), announces that it is "a national political party dedicated to a spirit of moderation based upon respect for human nature, seeking to advance in company with the common people through the energy and practice of reform." Among its fundamental policies are: (1) To work to establish a benevolent society in which both the prosperity of society as a whole and the happiness of the individual can be realized through a spirit of respect for the human being. (2) To promote a policy of independent and peaceful diplomacy. (3) To protect the present "peace" constitution of Japan and guard basic human rights. (4) To establish parliamentary democracy. At present the Komeito ranks second in size among the opposition parties. Its present chairman is Yano Junya.

**Nichiren Shoshu Soka Gakkai of America** - Nichiren Shoshu Soka Gakkai of America is the full name of an organization often referred to by the abbreviated title NSA. It was founded in the United States in 1960 by a small group of Soka Gakkai members living in America. In May 1963 it was granted formal recognition as a religious organization by the state of California under the name The Soka Gakkai of America. In December 1980 the name was changed to that listed above. The director of NSA is George M. Williams and its headquarters is located in Santa Monica, California.

**World Tribune** - An English language publication of the NSA or Nichiren Shoshu Soka Gakkai of America. It is devoted mainly to news of NSA activities and material that can help to bring about a better understanding of the Buddhist teachings of Nichiren Daishonin. Its chief editor is Mr. George M. Williams. The publication was founded in August 1964 and at present is a weekly.

# SOURCE MATERIAL

Sources for this research consisted of numerous interviews with Soka Gakkai officials in Japan and the United States in 1975-77 and 1984-87. There were also a considerable number of interviews with Soka Gakkai members throughout Japan. Published material consulted includes every issue of the Soka Gakkai News from 1976-86, many issues of the Seikyo Shimbun, and many other Soka Gakkai publications as well as numerous secondary sources.

## INTERVIEWS

Interviews were conducted on the dates indicated. In some cases additional meetings were held, but only the date of the initial interview has been given. Positions are those held by persons at time of interview. (SG = Soka Gakkai)

Akiya Einosuke
President, Soka Gakkai
3/20/87

Akiyama Tomiya
SG: Director, International Bureau
11/20/75

Aoki Tooru
SG: Vice-President
6/20/84

Harada Minoru
SG: Director, Student and Youth Divisions
8/8/76

Higuma Takenori
Author of book on Toda Josei
12/6/76

Eugene Hirahara
Official at NSA office - Washington, DC.

Ikeda Daisaku
SG: Former President
7/14/84

Kawada Yoichi
SG: Chief, Science Division
8/30/76

Kirimura Yasuji
SG: First Vice-Chief, Study Department
2/1/76

Guy McCloskey
Director, SE Region of NSA
12/17/86

Matsuoka Osamu
Managing Editor, Seikyo Shimbun
6/12/84

Murano Shenshu
Professor of Buddhism - Rissho University
4/1/76

Murata Kiyoaki
Former Editor of Japan Times
10/1/75

Nakane Chie
Anthropologist, Tokyo University
12/2/75

Nishiyama Shigeru
Professor of Sociology, Tokyo Kyoiku University
11/4/75

Shimada Yukio
Professor of International Law, Waseda University
7/1/84

Shiotsu Tohru
SG: Peace and Cultural Movement Office
6/19/84

Takikawa Masuo
SG: Deputy Director, International Bureau
2/21/76

Tsukamoto Akira
Journalist for Nippon Television
7/2/84

Ueda Masaichi
SG: Vice-President
6/12/84

Yamaguchi Hiromu
SG: International Bureau
12/1/75

Yamazaki Hisami
SF: Vice-President
8/4/76

Yano Junya
Secretary General, Komeito
7/30/84

Zhou Jinxiong
SG: International Bureau
6/17/84

# BIBLIOGRAPHY

Anesaki Masaharu, <u>Nichiren: The Buddhist Prophet</u>. Gloucester, MA.: Peter Smith, 1966.

Arai Kunio, "Why the Liberal Democrats Barely Survived,": in the <u>Japan Echo</u>, June, 1984.

<u>Asahi Evening News</u>, July 30, 1984.

<u>Asahi Nenkan</u>, 1986.

Bethel, Dayle M. <u>Makiguchi: The Value Creator</u>. Tokyo: Weatherhill, 1973.

Curtis, Gary. "NSA: Rekindling the American Spirit," <u>Japan Times</u>, August 14, 1976, pp. B5 and B7.

Fujiwara Hirotatsu, <u>I Denounce Soka Gakkai</u>. Tokyo: Nisson Hodo, 1960.

Harashima Takashi, <u>Sokagakkai</u> (The Soka Gakkai). Tokyo: Seikyo Shoten, 1970.

Higuma Takenori, <u>Toda Josei</u> (Toda Josei). Tokyo: Shin Jimbutsu Shoten, 1971.

Hori Yukio, <u>Komeitoron</u> (The Komeito). Tokyo: Aoki Shoten, 1973.

Ikeda Daisaku, "Answers to Questions on the Komeito," Komeito Series, 1968.

Ikeda Daisaku, <u>Buddhism: The Living Philosophy</u>. Tokyo: The East Publications, 1976.

Ikeda Daisaku,, <u>Complete Works of Daisaku Ikeda</u>, Vol. 1. Tokyo: Seikyo Press, 1968.

Ikeda Daisaku, <u>Guidance Memo</u>. Tokyo: Seikyo Press, 1966.

Ikeda Daisaku, <u>The Human Revolution</u>, vols. 1-4. Tokyo: The Seikyo Press, 1972-79.

Ikeda Daisaku, A Lasting Peace. Tokyo: Weatherhill, 1981.

Ikeda Daisaku, Lectures on Buddhism, Vols. 1-4. Tokyo: The Seikyo Press, 1962-67.

Ikeda Daisaku, Rissho Ankokuron Kogi (Lectures on Rissho Ankokuron). Tokyo: Sokagakkai, 1967.

Ikeda Daisaku, Seiji to Shukyo (Politics and Religion). Revised Ed. Tokyo: Ushio Shinsho, 1969.

Ikeda Daisaku, Watashi no Bukkyoken (My View of Buddhism). Tokyo: Daisan Bunmeisha, 1974.

Imai Masaharu and Nakao Takashi, Nihon Meiso Jiten (Dictionary of Famous Japanese Priests). Tokyo: Tokyodo Shuppan, 1976.

Inoue Nobutaka, Umi o Wattatta Nihon Shukyo (Japanese Religions Abroad). Tokyo: Kobundo, 1985.

Japan Times, August 14, 1976; July 6, 1984.

Japanese-English Buddhist Dictionary. Tokyo: Daito Shuppansha, 1965.

Kasahara Ichiro et al., Nihonshi (History of Japan). Tokyo: Sanseido, 1975 and 1981.

Kasahara Kazuo, Kakumei no Shukyo: Ikko Ikki to Sokagakkai (Revolutionary Religions: The Ikko Uprising and the Soka Gakkai). Tokyo: Jimbutsu Oraisha, 1964.

Kasahara Kazuo, Tenkanki no Shukyo. (Religion in Periods of Change). Tokyo: NHK Books, 1974.

Kato Bunno et al., trans. The Three-Fold Lotus Sutra. Tokyo: Weatherhill-Kosei, 1975.

Kato Bunno , Tenkanki no Shukyo (Religion in Periods of Change). Tokyo: Asoka Suppansha, 1965.

Makiguchi Tsunesaburo, Kachiron (Essay on Value Creation). Tokyo: The Soka Gakkai, 1953.

191

Makiguchi Tsunesaburo, The Philosphy of Value. Tokyo: Seikyo Press, 1964.

McFarland, H. Neil. The Rush Hour of the Gods. New York: Harper and Row, 1967.

Metraux, Daniel. The Religious and Social Philosphy of the Soka Gakkai. Unpublished doctoral dissertation, Columbia University, 1978.

Murano Senshu, Trans. The Lotus Sutra. Tokyo: Kyodo Obun Ctr., 1974.

Murano Senshu,, Trans. Nichiren's Nyorai Metsugo Go Gohyakusaishi Kanjin Honzonsho or the True Object of Worship Revealed for the First Time in the Fifth of the Five Century Periods After the Great Decease of the Tathagata. Tokyo: The Young East Association, 1954.

Muroo Tadashi, Soka Gakkai - Rissho Koseikai. Tokyo: Mainichichi Shuppansha, 1979.

Murata Kiyoaki. Japan's New Buddhism. Tokyo: Weatherhill, 1969.

Nichiren Shoshu International Center, A Dictionary of Buddhist Terms and Concepts. Tokyo: Nichiren Shoshu Int. Ctr., 1983.

Nichiren Shoshu, Major Writings of Nichiren Daishonin, Vol. 1. Tokyo: Nichiren Shoshu International Center, 1979.

Nakagawa Nisshi, Nichirenshugi no Joshiki (The Wisdom of Nichirenism). Kyoto: Heiraku-ji, 1970.

Newsweek, June 5, 1972.

The Nichiren Shoshu Sokagakkai. Tokyo: Seikyo Press, 1966.

Nishiyama Sigeru, "Nichiren Shoshu Sokagakkai ni okeru 'Honmon no Kaidan' ron no Hensen" (The Vicissitudes of the Kaidan Controversy of the Nichiren Shoshu Soka Gakkai) in Nichirenshu no Shomondai (The Various Problems of the Nichiren Sects), Nakano Takashi, Ed. Tokyo: Yuzankaku Shuppan, 1975. pp. 241-75.

192

Ohara Teruhisa et al., Soka Gakkai no Shucho: Seimei e no Funade (The Declaration of the Soka Gakkai: Mission Towards a Century of Life). Tokyo: Daisanbunmeisha, 1975.

Ono Tatsunosuke, Nichiren (Nichiren). Tokyo: Yoshikawakobunkan, 1974.

Rodd, Laurel L. Nichiren: Selected Writings. Honolulu: University of Hawaii Press, 1980.

The Soka Gakkai News. Nos. 22-216 (February, 1976-March, 1987).

Soka Gakkai, "In Pursuit of Lasting Peace." Pamphlet, 1983.

Soka Gakkai. (Youth Division of Aichi Prefecture), Tabemono: Genzai-Shorai (Food: Today and Tomorrow). Undated Pamphlet.

Soka Gakkai. The Soka Gakkai. Tokyo: The Soka Gakkai, 1983.

Soka Gakkai. (Youth Division), Peace is our Duty. Tokyo: Japan Times, 1982.

Suematsu Yoshinori, "Makiguchi Sensei to Buppo to no deaim" (Makiguchi's Encounter with Buddhist Law) in Daibyaku Renge (June, 1976), pp. 20-23.

Sugimori Koji, Kenkyu Soka Gakkai. Tokyo: Jiyusha, 1976.

Tamura Yoshiro and Miyazaki Eishu, Eds. Nihon Kindai to Nichirenshugi (Japanese Modernization and Nichirenism). Tokyo: Shunjusha, 1972.

Tamura Yoshiro. Nichiren (Nichiren). Tokyo: Shununsha, 1975.

Toda Josei, Essays on Buddhism. Tokyo: Seikyo Press, 1961.

Toda Josei, Kantogenshu (A Collection of Articles). Tokyo: The Soka Gakkai, 1960.

Toda Josei, Koenshu (A Collection of Lectures). Tokyo: The Soka Gakkai, 1960.

Toda Josei, Lecture on the Sutra. Tokyo: Seikyo Press, 1968.

Toda Josei, Ronbunshu (collected Works). Tokyo: The Soka Gakki, 1960.

Paul Varley, Japanese Culture: A Short History. New York: Columbia University Press, 1977.

Watanuki Joji, Politics in Postwar Japanese Society. Tokyo: Tokyo University Press, 1977.

White, James. The Soka Gakkai and Mass Society. Stanford: Stanford University Press, 1970.

# INDEX

# STUDIES IN ASIAN THOUGHT AND RELIGION